Columbia University

Contributions to Education

Teachers College Series

No. 601

AMS PRESS
NEW YORK

AN ANALYSIS OF THE
ACTIVITIES AND POTENTIALITIES
FOR ACHIEVEMENT OF THE
PARENT-TEACHER ASSOCIATION
WITH RECOMMENDATIONS

144756

BY
ELMER S. HOLBECK, Ph. D.

TEACHERS COLLEGE, COLUMBIA UNIVERSITY

CONTRIBUTIONS TO EDUCATION

NO. 601

PUBLISHED WITH THE APPROVAL OF
Professor Willard S. Elsbree, *Sponsor*

BUREAU OF PUBLICATIONS
Teachers College, Columbia University
NEW YORK CITY
1934

Library of Congress Cataloging in Publication Data

Holbeck, Elmer Scott, 1893–
    An analysis of the activities and potentialities for
achievement of the parent-teacher association.

    Reprint of the 1934 ed., issued in series: Teachers
College, Columbia University. Contributions to educa-
tion, no. 601.
    Originally presented as the author's thesis, Columbia.
    Bibliography: p.
    1. Parents' and teachers' associations--United States.
I. Title. II. Series: Columbia University. Teachers
College. Contributions to education, no. 601.
LC231.H6   1972   370.19'31   78-176870
ISBN 0-404-55601-9

Reprinted by Special Arrangement with Teachers
College Press, New York, New York

From the edition of 1934, New York
First AMS edition published in 1972
Manufactured in the United States

AMS PRESS, INC.
NEW YORK, N. Y.   10003

PREFACE

It is the purpose of this study to evaluate, in terms of accomplishment and potentialities for accomplishment, the aims, activities, program, and work of the Parent-Teacher Association. The development and growth of the Parent-Teacher Association have been marked by opposition and struggle. Much criticism has been heaped upon it. Many educators and lay citizens alike have viewed the movement with suspicion. Others have sought to promote and stimulate its growth, but largely through faith in its potentialities rather than from admiration of its actual accomplishment. Its diffusion of interests, its failure to achieve a clearcut relation with the educational system, its often poorly conceived and inefficient methods, have retarded and inhibited its influence and have given the casual observer only too much reason to believe that it had no importance.

This is not the whole story, however. The primary purpose of the organization—to coördinate the work of home and school for the welfare of the child—capitalizes a community of interest on the part of parents and teachers which has an enormously high emotional appeal. When to a purpose of such social significance is added the fact that the phenomenal number of over 1,500,000 individuals are officially recorded as members of Parent-Teacher Associations in this country, it is apparent that the organization deserves much more than superficial examination and that it probably has a potential importance of considerable magnitude.

It is, furthermore, one of the few examples in the United States of spontaneously initiated local community activity with volunteer leadership. It has weathered the vicissitudes of over seventy years of growth and expansion. It has had an influence on educational legislation, on public opinion regarding education and on the conception of the parent's rôle in education. Whether it will in the future rise to the full potency of its possible influence, depends to a great extent on the methods and techniques which the Associations work out for themselves in the next few years. It is the purpose of this study to present some recommendations for improving existing practices in this direction.

Difficult as it is to make an evaluation of an organization with such an unusual disparity between potentialities and achievements, it is distinctly worth while to attempt it at the present time. In the past a concerted effort was made to keep the work of the Associations unimportant and unobtrusive, but this evasive attitude cannot be justified in a period when education has become a science no less than an art. This movement, in spite of its obvious weaknesses, has become an enterprise with which the modern educator must reckon. It is time for its potentialities to be generally admitted and for educators to join with parents in working on ways and means of assisting the organizations to reach them. The successful integration of the work of this organization with the work of the school, where it has been accomplished, has promoted so definitely the welfare of the child and the community that, despite the numerous difficulties such an effort presents, it should be attempted more generally. It is hoped that the facts and recommendations here presented will serve in some measure to encourage the educators and parents who elect to embark on this adventurous experiment.

ACKNOWLEDGMENTS

THE author desires to acknowledge his indebtedness to Professor Willard S. Elsbree, for his constant assistance and inspiration during the writing of the dissertation. He wishes also to express grateful appreciation to Dr. Jesse H. Newlon and Dr. James R. McGaughy for their constructive criticisms and stimulating suggestions. To Mrs. Maria L. Rogers, formerly of the United Parents Association, whose many suggestions and criticisms were invaluable, the writer is extremely grateful. The author is also indebted to Mrs. Arthur C. Watkins, field secretary of the National Congress of Parents and Teachers for her many suggestions and careful reading of parts of the manuscript and to Dr. Julian E. Butterworth of Cornell University for his many constructive criticisms and suggestions found in his writings on Parent-Teacher Association work.

Without the coöperation of the National Congress of Parents and Teachers, United Parents Association, Virginia Coöperative Association and many other independent associations, the work would not have been possible.

Appreciation is also expressed to the following ten coöperating presidents in the field: Mrs. Johanna Mosenthal, New York City; Mrs. Alonzo Knapp, Port Chester, N. Y.; Mrs. H. H. Lieblich, Newark, N. J.; Mrs. Harry F. Maxman, Mountain View, N. J.; Mrs. Joseph V. Schnupp, East Port Chester, Conn.; Mrs. Joseph F. Schnugg, Hackensack, N. J.; Mrs. Robert Swank, Jackson Heights, L. I.; Mrs. Theodore Kuh, New York City; Mrs. H. E. Seim, Bridgeport, Conn.; and Mrs. E. P. Bodine, Fairfield, Conn.

To Mr. Jacob Theobald, Mrs. B. F. Lansworthy, First Vice President of National Congress of Parents and Teachers, Mrs. Adolph Kroll, President of Woodrow Wilson School Parent-Teacher Association, Passaic, N. J., Miss Isabel Haggerty, Supervisor, Passaic, N. J., Miss Thelma G. Paruta, Miss Florence B. Childs, Miss Alice D. Morgan, and Mr. Rudolph Graf, the author expresses his deep appreciation for their very helpful assistance.

To the hundred association presidents throughout the country and the many Parent-Teacher Association officials and educators, too numerous to mention, he feels especially obligated.

To his wife, Lydia S. Holbeck, for her assistance and unfailing inspiration and encouragement during the painstaking work of writing the dissertation, the author will always be grateful.

E. S. H.

CONTENTS

CHAPTER I

THE SCOPE OF THE STUDY

SINCE it is the purpose of this study to analyze the objectives, purposes, and functions of the Parent-Teacher Association, the plan of work followed has been, first, to study the historical development of the association since its inception, its organization, and relationship to the school and its publicity and finance activities; second, to analyze the actual relation existing between the conception of function and purpose held by the leaders in Parent-Teacher Association work and in educational thought and theory in the United States, and the activities engaging the attention of the local Associations.

Attention will be directed to the type of work done by ten Parent-Teacher Associations selected for case studies, and a chapter will be devoted to a proposed plan for unifying the program of an Association in a manner similar to the *Unit of Work* system now used so widely in the schools throughout the United States. There will also be included a list of specific recommendations designed to increase the efficiency and social value of the Parent-Teacher Association.

Since it appears that the major number of members of Parent-Teacher Associations in the United States have joined the National Congress of Parents and Teachers, which is the official national organization, close attention has been given to this body. But as some of the most interesting and original work in this field is carried on by local Associations which are not members of the National Congress, the available material relating to their activities has also been carefully studied.

The National Congress of Parents and Teachers, through its county and state branches, numbers 1,511,203[1] members of local Parent-Teacher Associations, organized in 20,000 units scattered throughout 47 states of the Union, Hawaii and Alaska. These units, composed of parents and teachers, are autonomous local Associations, organized in each school. Thousands of other units

[1]Figure quoted by National Congress of Parents and Teachers. Washington, D. C. 1931.

1

are affiliated in State Associations, independent of the National Congress of Parents and Teachers, such as the State Improvement League of Maine, the South Carolina School Improvement Association, the Virginia Coöperative Education Association; and decentralized independent units exist in every state in the Union. The National Congress of Parents and Teachers has been unable to estimate these independent units.[2] It has, however, made some attempt through its own units to assemble information about those independent Associations existing as separate or distinct units or as part of a larger group or council. The program of the independent groups and of the state federations mentioned above, is undoubtedly comparable in importance to that of the units which are members of the National Congress of Parents and Teachers, which for brevity will hereafter be referred to as the National Congress.

Data utilized for this study have been: Reports, programs and literature of the independent units and the State Associations, together with publications, proceedings, and reports of the National Congress and its state branches.

A questionnaire was sent to 275 Parent-Teacher Associations selected at random throughout the United States in order to obtain direct information about the status and working plan of typical groups. Of the 110 questionnaires returned, the information of 100 which were intelligently prepared was selected and used in this study. A personal intensive investigation of the work done by ten selected Parent-Teacher Associations in three different states was conducted by the author. The case studies of these ten Associations will be found in the body of the work, coupled with an evaluation of their social value to the community.

Other studies in the field, magazine articles, and check lists were also used in assembling facts and material. Many original data were assembled by the author during his personal observation and study of many Associations.

[2]See Appendix, Table A.

CHAPTER II

GROWTH AND DEVELOPMENT OF THE
PARENT-TEACHER ASSOCIATION

Our consideration of the growth and development of the Parent-Teacher Association will cover four aspects of the movement—one, the history of the early beginnings; two, its diffusion abroad; three, the formation of the National Congress; and, four, the recent developments which mark changes in its character and program. The Parent-Teacher Association movement, according to the most reliable accounts, seems to have had its beginnings in the United States as early as 1855. Following the development of the kindergarten, there arose a feeling that mothers and teachers could do more for the children by working together. This feeling was first expressed only in informal mothers' meetings, but it soon developed into more formal organizations such as Parents' Leagues, Mothers' Unions, Pre-School Circles, and Reading Councils, all of which were part of a movement which was wholly spontaneous and had no expressed philosophy. It simply filled a definite need felt by some parents and educators for a better understanding of the child in relation to school and society.

These isolated units in some states gradually felt the need for exchange of opinions, for the strength that comes from concerted action of many groups working together, and the result was the formation of state associations in Maine, South Carolina, Pennsylvania, Illinois, California, Virginia, Alabama, Oklahoma, and elsewhere.[1]

The Maine Improvement League is typical of a number of state associations in states whose population is predominately rural. It is concerned with the problems of rural schools and through its operation school grounds are improved and decorated. The South Carolina School Improvement Association no longer exists as a state unit but there are numerous independent associations scattered all over the state. The aim of this Association is the im-

---

[1]State School Improvement Association, Rural School Pamphlet No. 42, U. S. Bureau of Education, Washington, D. C., 1927.

3

provement of material and equipment through the raising and supplying of funds. With the help of this Association most of the schools are well housed and well equipped. In addition, a program for the consolidation of schools has been executed successfully by most of the state associations.

Another very flourishing and effective state organization is the Coöperative Education Association of Virginia, composed of 1,738 units and 82,762 members.[2] It was organized in 1904 to "advance social, spiritual, moral, physical, civic, and economic interests of the community." It claims to unite the official and unofficial leaders of the state in a great coöperative effort, by unifying all the educational forces with a view to utilizing their combined wisdom and strength in reinforcing the efforts of the state and local school authorities in the matter of perfecting the public school system of Virginia. A former executive secretary of the Association emphasizes the importance of its work in the following statement:

Through the leagues the latent forces of our State are stimulated into action. The power which makes the school go is the sentiment which exists in the community. From a few struggling organizations in 1904 there are now 1,833 leagues in the State of Virginia. During that time the amount of money spent in public education and school buildings has increased over 500 per cent. Training and salaries of teachers have also increased several hundred per cent. . . In every community there has been a loyal band of men and women with a vision of better things for their schools and communities, and it is this leaven that hath leavened our whole society.[3]

But thousands of local Parent-Teacher Associations never united with these state associations. This has been true in the larger cities. A similar condition exists in other urban areas. In some cities independent federations limited to the area have grown up. An example is the United Parents Associations of New York City, which numbers one hundred and fifty associations in its membership (1930).

The programs of these city federations may vary considerably in the different localities. Sometimes they are limited to monthly conferences and occasional work as a joint unit on special educational projects. The United Parents Associations above referred to have gone beyond this restricted program and furnish

[2]Includes 1,004 Junior leagues and 8,732 leagues for Adults. *The Community League News,* Richmond, Virginia, 1932.
[3]*Report.* Twentieth Anniversary of the Coöperative League of Virginia, 1924, Page 101

skilled assistance to local associations on all phases of local work, and have taken the leadership in assisting the member associations to carry on programs of parent education.

A new development in recent years has been the formation of parents' groups for the exclusive purpose of parent education. These exist in many cities along the Eastern seaboard and in some cases, as in Philadelphia, they have formed local branches of the Child Study Association of America.

Sometimes parents whose children attend private schools have formed a league devoted exclusively to the problems of such schools. Examples are the Parents League of New York and the Parents League of Brooklyn. There are others of the same type. It is extremely difficult to present briefly the many directions these groups have taken. The variation is almost bewildering. But enough has probably been said here to indicate both their variety and the characteristic all have in common — that of a nice adaptation to the specific needs of the members composing the groups.

When we come to the National Congress the picture is simplified immediately, as is always the case when an official organization is considered. In 1896, Mrs. Alice McLillan Birney conceived of a *Congress of Mothers.* This had as its objective the study of the care and training of children, and was the first official recognition on the part of parents that parenthood was a profession necessitating study and training. On February 17, 1897, Mrs. Birney's idea became a fact and the *National Congress of Mothers* was organized with Mrs. Birney as its first president. Its appeal was instantaneous, and state branches were organized everywhere and speedily affiliated with the national organization. Independent Parent-Teacher Associations already existing in Pennsylvania, Illinois, and California also joined forces with the national body.

At first it was the purpose of the Congress merely to organize groups of mothers for the study of the child. A few of these groups were organized in churches. Others were associated with the kindergartens or the public schools. Some were neighborhood groups. According to Mason,[4] the Parent-Teacher movement developed into types of Associations, all differing somewhat in membership and methods of work. The different types within the National Congress of Parents and Teachers are briefly classified

[4]Mason, M. S. *Parents and Teachers.* Ginn and Company, New York, 1928. Page 150.

under the following heads: Pre-school Associations; Parent-Teacher Associations in elementary schools; Parent-Teacher Associations in high schools; Mothers' Clubs; Fathers' Clubs; Study Circles; Parent-Teacher Associations in churches; and Parent-Teacher Associations in colleges.

But in time the Congress saw the necessity of associating in a helpful and intimate way the two social institutions exercising the most direct influence upon the child, the *home* and the *school*. There was therefore apparent a need for continuing the work into the elementary school and for joining in a common effort the elementary teachers as well as the mothers. To this end the Congress then entered upon a national movement for the organization of Parent-Teacher Associations. This phase of the work grew so rapidly that, in order that it might be directed more effectively, a special department in charge of it was created within the Congress.

At this point we may note the preponderance of elementary school organizations over all others.[5] This is partially accounted for by the fact that the elementary school is the most widely distributed educational agency; by the fact, also, that for many years the Congress emphasized elementary school organization; and perhaps it may also be explained by the fact that the elementary school child is at an age at which the mothers are easily interested in him and in his welfare.

In 1908 the name of the Congress was changed by vote to *The National Congress of Mothers and Parent-Teacher Associations*, and in 1915 the charter was amended to legalize this name. In 1924 the name was changed again, this time to that which it bears to-day, *The National Congress of Parents and Teachers*. This change was felt to be necessary because membership in the Congress is individual and because of the growth of interest on the part of fathers as well as mothers in the work of the Parent-Teacher Associations.[6]

Commenting on the inception of the Parent-Teacher Association movement, Butterworth[7] says: "Its original purposes included the education of parents for child development, the coöperation of home and school, the promotion of the kindergarten movement,

---

[5]See Appendix, Table B.
[6]*Handbook for Parent-Teacher Associations*. The National Congress of Parents and Teachers, 1931. Page 56.
[7]Butterworth, J. E. *The Parent-Teacher Association and Its Work*. The Macmillan Company, 1929. Page 7.

the securing of legislation for neglected and dependent children and the education of young people for parenthood."
Speaking of the potentialities of the movement, Mrs. Birney, the founder, said in her first address to the Congress in 1897:[8]

The age in which we live is a time for specialized work and organized effort. It has therefore seemed to us good that the highest and holiest of all missions, motherhood, the family interest upon which rests the entire superstructure of human life and the element which may be designated as the foundation of the entire social fabric, should now be the subject of our earnest, reverent, consideration.

This need of "earnest, reverent, consideration," expressed by Mrs. Birney and generally felt throughout the United States, was not, however, confined to the United States. Other countries soon followed the example set. But their work has so far not progressed beyond a stage comparable to the initial stages of the movement here.

Before turning to a consideration of the further development of the Parent-Teacher Association idea in America, let us consider briefly the movement as it is found in foreign countries.

Canada, following the example of the United States, initiated Parent-Teacher Associations throughout the provinces. Parent Councils provided for by law are found in Germany, Danzig, and Austria. Poland, Paraguay, Holland, Belgium, Bulgaria, and Australia all have officially recognized Parent Councils. Cuba has 1,373 associations of Parents, Neighbors, and Teachers. Mexico had a large number of isolated Parent-Teacher Associations but in 1928 these were formed into a large National Council. The investigation by the International Bureau of Education, Geneva, 1927–1928, shows in addition a widespread growth of private school associations. In England there is the Parents' National Educational Union, and in France the National Union of Parents and Teachers.

Despite this fairly large array of examples, it may nevertheless be stated that the movement in foreign countries is still in its infancy. The report of the International Bureau lists a number of reasons for the slow and unproductive growth of the movement in foreign lands. Among these are:

[8]*Twenty Years Work for Child Welfare, 1897–1917.* The National Congress of Parents and Teachers. Page 4.

1. Friction and discord due to lack of education and interest in pedagogical questions on the part of parents.

2. In *England* there are already too many societies and as a result schoolmasters are unwilling to accept advice or assistance from the parents.

3. In *Norway* the Supervising Committee of Parents is antagonistic to teachers.

4. In *India* a wide gulf separates the generations.

5. In *South Africa* educational authorities are already subject to public control.

6. In *France* politics, the breach between secondary and primary schools, and the ignorance of teachers as to the merits of school and home coöperation, all serve to militate against such a movement.

However, in the opinion of the writer, these reasons are superficial. The really important factor which has militated against the successful adoption of the American Parent-Teacher Association plan in foreign countries probably is the fact that the philosophy of the educational system in the United States differs radically from that which is held in foreign countries. It is built about a democratic ideal of education which found its first expression in the conception of the "Little Red Schoolhouse." From this "Little Red Schoolhouse" has developed a system of education in which each state sets minimum standards, and development and control are left largely to the local community. In foreign countries, on the other hand, there is a nationally integrated educational system with authority vested not in the community but in a national body. This difference in educational theory as well as a difference in social ideals makes it next to impossible successfully to adapt the American Parent-Teacher Association system to foreign countries. Full coöperation there between school and home would require considerable modification of educational philosophy, and although there is in foreign countries a stirring interest in the complete education of the whole child, the Parent-Teacher Associations there find themselves beset with difficulties which trouble the associations in the United States only slightly.

Typical of the rather superficial consideration given to the profound racial and cultural differences which have affected and will affect the development of this movement in foreign countries is this comment, made by a past president of the National Congress of

Parents and Teachers and President of the International Federation of Home and School, which was founded in Toronto in 1927:

We realize fully that each nation must work out its own programme, and we in the United States have no desire to claim that our plan is perfect or the one which everyone shall follow. But we do know by experience that it works well with a great variety of nationalities. We have in our National Congress groups speaking Spanish, Japanese, Russian, etc. So you see we have worked out something which is not only Anglo-Saxon but which is adaptable to many points of view.[9]

It is obvious to any sociologically trained observer that the foreign-speaking groups which have joined the Parent-Teacher Association in the United States are making an adaptation to American conditions, whereas in their own countries they might have behaved quite differently.

Following its inception here the movement was greeted with great enthusiasm. Something of this and something of the underlying philosophy, the early objectives, and proposals, are seen in the first effort to enlist support for its cause. This appeal was sent to all the leading women's clubs in the country. It follows:

The first National Congress of Mothers will be held in Washington, D. C., February 17, 18, 19, 1897. Washington has been selected as the most fitting place for such an assemblage because the movement is one of national importance and because the city offers many advantages in other ways.

The originator of the present project, believing in the necessity for organized and earnest effort on the part of the mothers of the land concerning questions most vital to the welfare of their children and the manifold interests of the home, presented the subject at some of the Mothers' meetings at Chautauqua in the summer of 1895. The earnest enthusiasm with which it was received made it evident that the thought needed only to be disseminated in order to be quickly accepted and acted upon by hosts of conscientious, thinking women throughout the world, and to result in a centralization of their power toward the accomplishment of great and necessary reforms in the interests of humanity.

It is universally admitted that feminine influence has been a mighty factor for good in all ages and, therefore, incalculable benefit may be expected from the assemblage of many women for the interchange of views and the study of home problems which can be solved by women alone.

It is proposed to have the Congress consider subjects bearing upon the better and broader spiritual and physical as well as mental training of the young, such as the value of kindergarten work and the extension of its prin-

---

[9]*Results of an Investigation Undertaken by the International Bureau of Education, Geneva, 1927-28.* Page 4.

ciples to more advanced studies, a love of humanity and of country, the
physical and mental evils resulting from some of the present methods of our
schools, and the advantages to follow from a closer relationship between the
influence of the home and school.[10]

Following this appeal the National Congress grew steadily.
In 1900 seven states were affiliated with the movement. By 1920
every state with the single exception of Nevada had a comprehensive state organization. The growth in membership also is note-
worthy. In 1912 there were 31,672 members. In 1921 membership was 278,721, and by 1931 it had grown to 1,511,203, with
Associations numbering over 20,000.[11] But, as noted above, it has
not by any means included all of the Parent-Teacher Associations
in its membership.

The history of the Parent-Teacher Association cannot be written
without a brief glance at the cultural setting in which it has developed. The scope of this study naturally permits no more than
a mere enumeration of some of the factors which have reacted
upon this movement. The year 1855, when the first mothers'
clubs were formed, is close to the period from which we usually
date the emergence of those profound changes in our national
industrial life which have completely altered our material environ-
ment, namely, the onset of the Civil War. These material
changes, however, were not the only ones. Population concentration in big cities, revolutionary changes in the status of women,
new concepts of government and social life, new forms of entertainment and amusement, have marked this period. Educational
theory and practice, also, have reflected these changes and have in
turn influenced their character.

The change in the status and interests of women and the new
educational theories are all that concern us directly in this study.
Women were largely set free from the drudgery of pioneer days.
Their new leisure was immediately utilized in widening their
horizons. Most of this early effort took place through the women's
clubs. They began to get a picture of the complexity of modern
civilization of which, when safely immured within the four walls
of their homes, they had been blissfully ignorant. They began to
feel responsible for remedying the ugly aspects of this civilization.

[10]*Through the Years.* National Congress of Parents and Teachers, Washington, D. C., 1930.
Page 13.
[11]A table showing the growth of the Congress units may be obtained from the National Congress of Parents and Teachers, 1201 16th Street N. W., Washington, D. C.

Their leaders demanded the suffrage, universal peace, abolition of child labor, prohibition of drinking, and so forth. Those women who were not drawn into a consideration of world affairs felt profoundly uneasy about the changes which affected their homes and their children's welfare. New educational theories were in the air which they did not understand and toward which they often were antagonistic. The motion picture, amusement parks, dance halls, were forms of entertainment which removed their children from the narrow neighborhood circle and drew them away from the shelter of the home attitudes. It became more and more difficult not to take into account a host of factors which affected the children and of which the parents had no first-hand knowledge. The impact of these new community conditions reacted on the children and made life infinitely more complex for the growing child and the adolescent than had perhaps ever been true in the world before. He found himself at the mercy of conflicting attitudes of social behavior without any stabilizing center in which they could be reconciled. All these conditions made, and still make, motherhood a difficult and a most exacting rôle.

In 1855 it must have seemed a simple matter to bring mothers and teachers together to study what little was then known of child psychology. As the century wore on and the complexities of life and education became ever greater and women began to know more about the social conditions of the time, this simple purpose was lost sight of in the excitement of using the new influence women found in their hands to reform the world. It was just before the close of the century that the National Congress of Mothers was formed and it did not escape the reformist spirit which was so sharply exhibited all through our national life during the first decade of the twentieth century. Indeed, child study itself was converted into a crusade! In the March, 1898, issue of the *Mothers Magazine*, Volume 1, we find a statement which admirably illustrates the transformation which had taken place:

Every man and woman who begins to comprehend the sacred obligations due to helpless little children and who longs for their harmonious development, possesses the attributes which will lead him or her to forward this development. Cannot all of us at the close of this nineteenth century be filled with the spirit of the crusaders, with that zeal and fire which made each individual in those times a soldier in the cause of Christ? No man then waited for orders from superior officers, no organization could meet his need, no soldier could fill his place. In such a cause there could be no substitute and thus it should be in this crusade against ignorance and indifference.

From that confusion of purpose the Congress has never freed itself. Although we find in the speeches and writings of the time an assumption that it was the function of the Parent-Teacher Association to educate the parent so that he might better be able to cope with existing conditions and meet more intelligently the problem of rearing a child in a changing civilization, nevertheless the most extensive diffusion of interests was tolerated which had nothing to do with this purpose and function. For example, the Congress in 1926 continued to state its objects as:

1. To promote child welfare in home, school, church, and community; to raise the standards of home life; to secure more adequate laws for the protection of women and children.

2. To bring into closer relation the home and the school that parents and teachers may coöperate in the training of the child; to develop between educators and the public such united effort as will secure for every child the highest advantages in physical, mental, moral, and spiritual education.[12]

But when it came to action, it is too apparent that the Congress was not carrying out these purposes as energetically as it might have done. A concrete illustration is obtained by examining impartially its plan of departmental organization. This shows a great emphasis on expansion activities and a wide diversity of interests not related to the stated purposes. The six departments[13] organized by the national federation were:

1. Organization: Child Welfare Day, Congress Publications, Membership.

2. Extension: Parent-Teacher Associations in Colleges, in High Schools, in Grade Schools, in Churches, Study Circles, Pre-School Circles.

3. Public Welfare: Citizenship, Juvenile Protection, Legislation, Motion Pictures, Recreation, Safety.

4. Education: Art, Humane Education, Illiteracy, Kindergarten, Extension, Music, School Education, Student Loan Fund, Scholarships.

5. Home Service: Children's Reading, Home Economics, Home Education, Spiritual Training, Standards in Literature, Social Standards, Thrift.

6. Health: Child Hygiene, Mental Hygiene, Physical Education, Social Hygiene.

---

[12]National Congress of Parents and Teachers, *Handbook*, 1926. Page 1.

[13]The standing committees and their grouping in departments vary as need arises but this list illustrates the way in which the Congress is seeking to meet the permanent requirements of childhood.

The diffusion of interests and attachment to aims not directly related to its purpose is also illustrated by the set of resolutions adopted by the National Congress in 1926:

1. Complete enforcement of prohibition.
2. A program of education to protect children by law and public opinion (Child Labor).
3. A program for World Peace.
4. A Federál department of education with a secretary in the President's Cabinet.
5. Extension of the Shepherd-Towner Act beyond June, 1927.
6. Narcotic education as a means of combatting the menace of drug addiction.
7. A commission on illiteracy and strict endorsement of the compulsory education law.
8. Reaffirming of position regarding salacious literature, continuing to arouse public protest against the sale of objectionable magazines.
9. Favor establishment of National Teachers' Day for the recognition of teachers.
10. Program of safety and thrift education and a diversified recreational program which shall contribute to the moral education of youth.

This diffusion of interest and relative neglect of child study was not only tolerated by the leaders of the Congress and by leaders of independent bodies as well, but by the educators themselves. When the Congress moved in 1913 to bring educators to a realization that the Parent-Teacher Association could be an aid to the school in the education of the child, it met with resistance.[14] Says Mrs. B. F. Langworthy:

It was curious to see the reaction of the school people to this movement. They were in many instances afraid of the onslaught of interested parents, mostly mothers, and cast about to find activities that should keep them busy and out of the mischief of trying to run the schools. It was a new interest to parents and it went to the heads of many of them whose resentment against new methods and new studies had been seething for a long time, no one having taken the trouble to make them understand them. There were undoubtedly many cases of interference and trouble-making, a difficulty that we have been trying, by education, to live down.[15]

[14]A conference was held in 1913 by the National Congress at the mid-winter meeting of the Department of Superintendence of the National Education Association, marking an important step toward a better understanding between the schools and the Congress. These conferences, held almost every year since then, have done much good in making the Congress known to educational leaders and securing the backing of the school system for Parent-Teacher Associations.

[15]Vice-President of the National Congress of Parents and Teachers, 1932. (In a letter directed to the writer).

As a result of this feeling on the part of the educators, the activities of the local Associations were directed into new and in many ways less important fields. They turned to a large extent to the task of raising money for the purchase of school equipment, to the arrangement of entertainments, and to other non-educational activities. There was little room left in their schedule for the study of parent and child problems. There were still some few good Associations in the more progressive schools and communities, but the original purpose of the movement which, however vaguely stated, was the education of parents in order that they might build up a better world for their children and consequently build better children, was held in abeyance.

Meantime, however, the educational world has evolved a new philosophy of education as a twenty-four hour a day process, and while unwilling perhaps two decades ago to see in the Parent-Teacher Association a medium for realizing this concept, now generally accept it as such. Educators to-day are stating more clearly and more imaginatively than leaders of the movement ever did the potentialities the organization bears within it. Says Moehlmann:

Any organization with so large a membership is bound to make its influence felt in both state and nation. An association with an emotional stimulus such as the Parent-Teacher Association contains, represents a potency that rises far beyond that of a group associated for business or ordinary purposes. In a large sense the Parent-Teacher Association is distinctly a public relation agency made necessary by the complications of our existing social organizations.[16]

Newlon has stated the case even more strongly:

The Parent-Teacher Association represents an effort on the part of the home and the school to study together their joint educational responsibilities. Child study associations, clinics of one kind or another, experiments with parent education classes, have risen to cope with these problems. I shall assert again the belief that I have expressed on former occasions—that the movement to bring school and home together in the study of their common problems represents one of the three or four most important movements in what is commonly regarded as one of the most creative periods in American education.[17]

---

[16]Moehlmann, A. B. "Defining Rights and Duties of Parent-Teachers Associations." *Nation's Schools*, June, 1931. Page 55.
[17]Newlon, Jesse H. "The Rôle of the Public School in Parent Education." An address delivered at the Biennial Conference of the National Council on Parent Education, Washington, D. C., 1930. Page 84.

The growing appreciation of adult education has had its impact on the attitude with which the efforts of the Parent-Teacher Association are at present viewed. Hart expresses the new attitude when he says:

> Any movement or institution that proposes to help men and women find some new increment of knowledge or understanding or skill or ability through their own hard efforts is socially valuable and should be supported whether it comes within the scope of "standard" institutions or not. Wherever men and women are struggling with the attempt to understand to-day whether in study groups, in library reading and research rooms, in general conversation, or in silence of individual meditation, there a university is in operation and the future is in process.[18]

While the Parent-Teacher Association movement was being diverted from its early purpose of child study, that purpose was adopted, developed and expanded in the study groups of the Child Study Association of America and many other unrelated groups. This also was a spontaneous organization, brought into being to satisfy the needs of mothers with a desire to study their children. The study groups developed outside the school, however, and therefore did not suffer the cramping experience of the Parent-Teacher Associations, and, since they were never tempted to expand for numbers only, they did not suffer much from the reformist impulse. This movement for parent education grew steadily until in 1925 a National Council on Parent Education was formed, which drew all the hitherto independent groups together for counsel and discussion. This body has in turn influenced the program of the National Congress by emphasizing the great importance of parent education in Parent-Teacher Associations. Other factors may have been the work of independent organizations, such as the United Parents Associations of New York City which in 1925 adopted a program which made child study the primary purpose of the organization. There are a few other examples of the kind. Whether because of these particular stimuli or others it is impossible to say, but in 1929 the National Congress with the help of foundation funds established a department of parent education with a secretary in charge for an experimental period of three years, to encourage its groups to study child psychology and child needs under competent leadership. The final stage of its work—the one

[18]Hart, J. K. *Adult Education.* Thomas Y. Crowell Company, New York, 1927. Page 297.

in which we now find ourselves—therefore represents a distinct step forward as well as a return to the earlier ideals of the Congress.

Dr. McAndrew in editorial comment quotes Mrs. Mason regarding the revised conception of the function of the Congress:

> It is our particular function not only to call attention to the value of all organized efforts to protect and educate the child, but also to provide a channel through which specialized information may reach fathers, mothers, and other citizens who deal with children.[19]

It is evident from this statement that the Congress has by no means abandoned its earlier position as an organization for getting things done even when it recognizes its responsibility as an agency for parent education. Whether or not it would be desirable for it to do so is not at all certain. The two purposes, with skillful management, can be made to run together, and no one could deny the value of the pressure which interested educated parents could bring to bear upon the educational system. The new type of educator does not dread this pressure as his predecessor did, as instanced by McAndrew, who says:

> Obtrusiveness is not as bad as indifference on the part of the community. . . . The Parent-Teacher Association organizes and leads toward the support of the schools those citizens who, however traditional their ideas of the purpose of the schools may be, have the strongest natural interest in them— that of parental devotion to children.[20]

All these various points of view, even on slight examination, show conflicting tendencies. The Parent-Teacher Association still has a host of problems to work out. It must consider ways and means of integrating its function as an agency for parent education with that of acting in appropriate ways to support and further the work of the schools. Perhaps this can never be done satisfactorily to all concerned but there certainly exists a need for both functions. The schools need the support of interested citizens in many crises; they cannot do their work without money and the taxpayers must vote the money. They cannot gain general acceptance for innovations and new methods without the support and understanding of the parents and other citizens. Moreover, the child needs an understanding, trained parent as never before in history, and the

[19]McAndrew, William, Editorial Comment. *School and Society*, Vol. 29, June 1, 1929. Page 715.
[20]*Ibid.* Page 714.

school cannot expect maximum results from its work unless it is supported at home by intelligent parents. The school and the home are irrevocably bound together in this civilization.

Realizing this, the school has before it the problem of working out such a relationship to the Parent-Teacher Association that the two institutions can function smoothly and without friction. More specific reference is made in Chapter II regarding the possible coöperation between the schools and the Parent-Teacher Association. The problem is complex and many experiments will have to be made before any final satisfactory solution is found, if ever. But every interested educator and every intelligent leader of the Parent-Teacher Association can help toward this solution.

E. C. Lindeman[21] has given some thought to this problem and feels that the manner in which the school should share in the parent education process is one for considerable debate. He says:

In some sections of the country, the situation seems entirely ripe for the incorporation of parent education within the established public education system, in others it seems equally clear that the most effective form of organization is one which preserves the voluntary elements in the movement, in still others it seems possible and advisable to combine these two types of organization.

The possibility of setting up in an educational system a department of Parent Education to work jointly with all other phases of Child Education should receive consideration from the various communities in the country. It is not, however, without danger. The determining factor in initiating such a scheme will of course be financial support and this probably should be public and not private. The acceptance of such a plan should result only when the following items have received careful consideration:

1. The danger of creating such a plan for a community not ready for it.
2. Adjustment to type of community.
3. Clarification and coördination of all functions concerned with Parent Education.
4. Type of leadership available.

Another suggestion foreshadowing possible future developments comes from Dr. Newlon:

[21]Lindeman, E. C. "Sociological Aspects of Parent Education," *Journal of Educational Sociology*. Vol. 5, April 1932. Page 505.

I am firmly convinced that the time has come when a highly trained professional leadership must be made available in this field (i.e., in the field of coöperation between the school and the Parent-Teacher Association). Every school system of any size should have on its staff persons charged with the responsibility of studying the family in its relation to the education of children, specialists who can skillfully and informally foster the work of parent education and similar groups.

Such a department should be a service department and not an administrative or supervisory department. Skillful leadership will informally assist parents and teachers in the study of their problems, rather than dictate or administer. It is impossible to foresee with any clarity what forms of coöperation will be set up. There is already available a considerable body of knowledge which should be placed at the disposal of parents and teachers, and needs to be greatly extended by research. The school should draw from the social sciences, from sociology, anthropology, economics as well as medicine and psychology, much tested knowledge pertinent to the education of parents and to the functioning of school and home.[22]

With these suggestions, which mark the latest development of educational thought concerning the Parent-Teacher Association, we can conclude this brief history of an organization which has reflected so many of the larger currents of American social life and seems likely in the future to become an intimate part of our entire educational structure.

SUMMARY

In considering the history of the Parent-Teacher Association, we find that it presents a number of features of great interest. In the first place, it arose as a spontaneous answer to a genuine need felt by parents and educators to obtain a better knowledge of the child in relation to school and society. There has never at any time been anything forced or artificial about its expansion, yet in the course of seventy years it has had a steady, and of recent years a phenomenal, growth in size.

Any organization with such a long history is bound to have changed its conceptions and ideals. Yet on the whole the Parent-Teacher Association has remained remarkably consistent. Although from the turn of the century the Associations began to lose sight of their primary purpose, which to-day we call parent education, because of the pressure of the social ideals of the time which stimulated women to throw their strength against any and

[22]Newlon, Jesse H. *Op. cit.*

all abuses of which they became aware, nevertheless, in spite of an immense and regrettable diffusion of energies over the whole social field, the primary purpose lay latent; it was not completely lost.

The movement has been powerfully affected not only by the social currents of the period, but by the attitudes of school administrators. For a long time the practical educators, who feared a flood of ill-advised and useless criticism and who were jealous of their prerogatives, made an attempt to keep the work of the Associations out of the schools. The efforts of the local units were directed into money-raising activities and other fields which had no connection with the original need which had brought the organization into being. It is this situation which to-day keeps the work of the Parent-Teacher Associations in foreign countries for the most part valueless and which still weakens to a great extent the effort being made in the United States.

In our day, however, because of the emergence of many new factors, among them a changed concept of education, educators and parents alike are looking upon this organization with fresh vision. The leaders in modern education have many of them accepted their responsibility for developing the potentialities of the Parent-Teacher Association, and thus it appears that with their assistance the Association can move forward to a higher level of achievement.

CHAPTER III

ORGANIZATION OF PARENT-TEACHER ASSOCIATION AND ITS RELATION TO SCHOOL ADMINISTRATION

PLAN OF ORGANIZATION

THE Parent-Teacher Association is always an autonomous, self-governing, self-supporting organization made up of the parents of the children attending a particular school,[1] except when the parents of a group of schools band together for the same purpose. This practically never happens in the Associations connected with public schools. Examples are occasionally found of such a type of organization for private schools.[2] The officers are usually a president, one or more vice-presidents, a secretary, and a treasurer. Any parent of a child in the school is eligible for membership. In some schools membership includes both parents. Some schools accept parents only for full membership; in the majority of schools, however, teachers and other faculty members are solicited to join. In the latter case one or more teachers are usually given offices in the organization, the remainder of the officers being drawn from the parents. Officers are always elected by the membership and the usual stipulation is that no person may serve for more than two consecutive terms. Exception to this rule is sometimes made for the treasurer and the treasurer is often a teacher.

Committees are usually appointed or elected for specific projects. In Associations which do not admit teachers to full membership, those whose advice is needed for such projects are usually made ex-officio members of the committees.[3]

Those local units which join a centralized body do so in one of two ways—either by affiliating as a unit with the central organiza-

---

[1] Exceptions are such groups organized in connection with churches, settlement houses and other philanthropic enterprises, but as these have practically no bearing on the present study, they are ignored in this chapter. They present no interesting modifications of the form of organization.

[2] Cf. Chapter I.

[3] The United Parents Associations of New York City recommends this plan to its members. In such Associations, the principal sits as an ex-officio member of the Executive Committee, which plans all the work.

tion, or by joining it as individuals in a group. This latter plan is the one adopted for admission to the National Congress. Such individual membership also makes the members of these units automatically members of the state branches of the National Congress where these exist.

All state organizations of the National Congress are bound to uniformity by its by-laws. There is, however, some variation in the details in which the finer points of organization are carried out. Article 12 of the By-Laws of the National Congress indicates to some degree the extent to which the National Congress brings about uniformity in its branches. Thus,

SECTION 3: Each state or branch shall elect a president, one or more vice presidents, one or more secretaries, a treasurer, and such other officers as it may find necessary. Each state branch shall be authorized to adopt rules for the transaction of its business provided they do not conflict with the by-laws of the National Congress. The state by-laws shall be approved by a committee of the National Board of Managers.

The State Board of Managers shall consist of the officers of the state branch, the district presidents (or, where there are no districts, county presidents), the chairmen of standing committees, the chairmen of committees-at-large and such others as may be approved by a committee of the National Board appointed for that purpose. No person shall serve on the state board of managers in more than one capacity; this shall not apply to district or county presidents whose term will expire within six months after the state election.

SECTION 10: Each state branch shall, in so far as possible, provide for state standing committees to correspond with the national standing committees. It shall be the duty of the state committee to endeavor to carry out the plans submitted by the like committee of the National Congress.

However, provision has been made in the Congress for elasticity in the organization of districts within the state or councils within the city or community. Eleven states have no district organization. Chart A[4] shows the state organization of New Jersey where local association members through conventions are directly responsible to the state. Chart B[5] shows the relation of national committees to state, district, council, and local committees. State branches may be organized with a membership aggregating 500 when the state has ten local units whose dues have been paid to the National Congress.

The Convention, which is the governing body of the national organization, formulating all its policies, is held annually at a

[4]See Appendix, Chart A.   [5]See Appendix, Chart B.

place fixed by the National Board of Managers. Delegates selected are: State President and three state officers, or the alternates, and one additional delegate for every thousand members in good standing. The State Board of Managers authorizes this selection.

Chart C[6] shows the unit of organization in the national body. In the National Congress office there are forty workers, including twenty-seven paid workers, of whom seven are division secretaries, one a general secretary and the six others in charge of Education, Research, Publicity, Summer Round-Up, Publications, and Field Work, as outlined on Chart E.[7] In addition to these divisions, the official publication of the National Congress of Parents and Teachers, *Child Welfare Magazine*, has its office on the same floor. Its staff includes thirteen persons, eleven staff workers under the direction of a business and a circulation manager. The Parent Education work of the National Congress of Parents and Teachers is also conducted from this office. The staff is the chairman of the Committee on Parent Education and a secretary.

The National Congress of Parents and Teachers has adopted specific recommendations[8] governing organization and program by which local Associations may become "standard" or "superior" Associations. These unfortunately encourage local units to pursue many different types of activity and promote a uniformity of activity among the local units which does not permit an adequate consideration of local problems. In Chapter V we shall discuss the purposes and functions of the Parent-Teacher Association, and in the light of these we can see the importance of encouraging a flexibility which will enable each local unit to evolve a program of work based on its own major problems.

Chart E indicates the great number of activities engaging the interest of the National Congress of Parents and Teachers. From a consideration of this chart one is led to believe that if fewer activities of major importance are considered desirable for local units, then the national organization should consolidate its interests to include only activities which may be used by a local unit in the study of problems peculiar to that community.

Chart D[9] indicates the general relationship of the Parent-Teacher

[6]See Appendix, Chart C.

[7]See Appendix, Chart E.

[8]*Report for Standard and Superior Associations*, 1931–32. National Congress of Parents and Teachers.

[9]See Appendix, Chart D.

Association to our educational system. The writer feels that the position of the Parent-Teacher Association is too obscure. For stability and prestige, its rights should be defined by the boards of education.[10] Its relationship to the school should be "extra-legal," but the Parent-Teacher Association must occupy a place in our educational system which will encourage it to assist in the effective solution of educational problems. The writer feels that the Parent-Teacher Association, properly placed and encouraged by the educational system, will not be likely to attempt to dictate policies and interfere with the work of the school. The instances of such interference can usually be traced to a confusion on the part of the members of the Parent-Teacher Association in regard to its function and often to ignorance of the purpose of the educational policies they attempt to combat. Where the school authorities have adopted a policy of keeping the parents informed of the general purpose and philosophy behind educational methods, this particular kind of friction has been practically eliminated. There are always unreasonable parents, because unreasonableness is common to human nature in general, but this trait causes as much trouble in schools where no Parent-Teacher Association exists as in schools where parents are organized. The writer, for example, found in a study of 125 Associations little of what might be called interference. Butterworth found in a study of the records of 887 business sessions only three or four cases of what might be counted as interference.[11]

MEMBERSHIP

Any parent may become a member of the Parent-Teacher Association in his child's school. He may continue to be a member long after his child has left school. Some organizations even extend membership to any interested citizen in the community whether he has children in the school or not; but this plan has dangers as it admits self-seeking politicians whose interests differ from those of the parents. The size of the membership in any Association seems to depend upon the vitality and energy put into the program of work. Some organizations include one hundred per cent of the parents in the organization, but this is rare, mem-

[10]The United Parents Associations of New York City has made an attempt to accomplish this. See "A Contribution to the Theory and Practice of Parents Associations," N. L. Rogers, 1931. Page 60.

[11]Butterworth, J. E. *Op. cit.*

bership sometimes falling as low as between three and ten per cent of the parents of a school. In one hundred Parent-Teacher Associations selected at random the range of membership was 7 to 1,200. The National Congress reports that more than fifty per cent of its local units have a membership ranging from 24 to 90 persons. It also reports an average membership of 45.[12] Butterworth[13] found that in cities with less than 2,500 population the median for nine states was 47, and that the median size increased proportionately with the size of the school. It is significant that all studies of the organization that have been made so far show less interest on the part of men than of women. Also school faculties have been somewhat slow to increase their membership in the Association. But at present more and more schools are showing one hundred per cent membership. There is no limit to the size of the membership, except the registration of any particular school. Large Associations by the use of committees function as effectively as smaller units.

The National Congress opens its membership to individuals not members of local units and permits any person interested in the aims and objects of the Congress to become an active or life member upon payment of dues.

The state and national organizations usually influence the formation of committees in the local units. Local units may appoint any committees necessary to carry on their work but the suggestions of the state are usually so all-inclusive that they are adopted. Chart F[14] represents graphically the duties of the members and the committees on which they serve. Independent units which have no connection with the National Congress are often charged with duties and responsibilities similar to this set-up.

Turnover in membership is extremely high. The mortality is partially offset by the addition of new members. In 1932, according to the National Congress of Parents and Teachers, there were 1,151,918 members in the grade school associations, while in the junior and senior high school associations there were 134,769. As a result of this study, the writer concludes that much of the turnover in membership may be charged to lack of interest, due to:

[12]*Special Report of National Congress of Parents and Teachers*, 1931 (305–932-GS.)
[13]Butterworth, J. E. *Op. cit.*
[14]See Appendix, Chart F.

1. Inadequate program of activity.
2. Objectives of Parent-Teacher Association not understood; parents are not sure of the efficacy of the work of the Association.
3. Pupil membership in school not constant.
4. No personal responsibility for membership.
5. No extensive study group plan to provide for individual needs of parents.

Minor reasons given by Association officers are:
1. Lack of time.
2. Political interference.
3. Friction.
4. Change of residence.
5. Meetings held at inconvenient times.
6. Lack of social intercourse.

MEETINGS

The number of meetings varies with the organization. Golden[15] found that the median in one hundred Associations was 8.61. In the present study the median in one hundred Associations was found to be 8.25. The range was four to twelve for regular meetings during the school year. In addition to regular meetings, however, many special meetings are held to provide for study groups and the solution of particular problems. The range of special meetings is four to twenty-four yearly. Many of these are not attended by the entire membership but are meetings of smaller groups to discuss problems relative to their needs. From observation and study the writer noted that the strongest Associations have a systematic program carried out at all regular meetings, supplemented by group meetings at regular intervals. Such Associations usually plan activities which are cumulative, organized under a large unit of work, and such a plan requires group meetings in order to reach definite objectives that have been adopted. Any organization which confines itself merely to large regular meetings accomplishes little.

METHODS OF ORGANIZING LOCAL ASSOCIATIONS

Since the formation of the local Parent-Teacher Association is usually due to spontaneous local initiative taken by relatively

[15]Golden, Emma. *The Present Status of the Parent-Teachers Associations in North Dakota.* The University of Minnesota, 1930. Page 57.

untrained persons, it is most unusual to find complete records dealing with the precise steps which have brought the present organizations into existence.   These first steps are, however, likely to be all-important for the future of the organization.   If petty political forces seize the leadership at the start, the organization is thereafter likely to be used as a tool to build up prestige by some aspirant who wishes to rise from the political ranks.   If unreasonable and narrow-minded persons with zeal and aggressiveness (and the combination is not unusual) become the first officers and committee chairmen, the organization within a short time often finds itself in trouble with the principal.   In neither case is a constructive policy and program of value to the majority of parents likely to be undertaken, for this involves disciplined intellectual effort and an imaginative approach at variance with the interests of this type of leader.

Since the National Congress is, in the minds of the general public, the official source of authoritative information regarding all phases of parent-teacher work, it would naturally be assumed that it would be prepared to give detailed advice on the formation of Associations, advice which would warn against the above pitfalls and many other avoidable mistakes.   Unfortunately, such is not the case.   It limits itself to the issuance of a small leaflet on organization, which is of a highly general character, and a set of by-laws for new Associations.   Since the future value and prestige of the local Association depend upon the right kind of start, this lack of official information regarding methods of organizing is serious. This question deserves more consideration from the Congress than has been given to it in the past.

The United Parents Associations of New York City, recognizing this need, has suggested methods to its local units which indicate the kind of help the National Congress could give.   This federation suggests[16] that in organizing a local Association it has been found highly advisable that a definite need of the organization be discovered in the community and that that need be discovered by the parents, the prospective members.   Probably the most successful method of initiating the project has been to hold several meetings of interested parents and, working through committees, to discuss local problems and needs.   Thus the aims and objectives of the organization are clearly defined and understood in the beginning.

[16]*The How and Why of a Parents Association.*   United Parents Associations, 1930.   Page 17.

When the group is brought to a realization that their problems can best be solved by an Association under efficient, unselfish leadership, then it may safely bring about plans for definite organization. The seriousness of the work and the type of activity that a Parent-Teacher Association is expected to put into operation are more clearly understood if the Association takes form under the influence of capable and thoughtful leadership. Until such leadership can be found, it is best to delay organization. Here the school principal can play an important part which calls for tact and skill. He can always bring about the formation of an organization but his efforts should be indirect, the result of influence and suggestion which gradually build up in the parents a belief that such an organization would help to solve the problems peculiar to both school and home. The initial steps had best be taken by the parents. Many school principals, actuated by the best motives and eager to help the parents of the school, have found that an organization too quickly developed and formalized soon falls apart. A rather long period of incubation[17] and patient education is required before sufficiently large numbers of parents can be made to realize the potentialities of an Association of the best type and before the proper unselfish leadership can be found.

In the one hundred Associations studied by the author it was found that only forty per cent of them had been initiated by parents. Also, instead of the careful procedure described above it was found that Associations are often organized on the spur of the moment to meet some special emergency which the Association is suddenly conceived as all-powerful to cope with. Instead of being the result of thoughtful, reasoned promotion, they spring into being during the violence of protest against a real or fancied grievance on the part of a small group of parents in a school. Nor is such ill-considered action always due to the shortsightedness of parents. Too many school principals are very likely to ignore the possibilities of a Parent-Teacher Association until they find their requests for a pet project meeting with resistance from the educational authorities. Then they resort to forming an organization of parents for the purpose of strengthening demands for additions to school equipment or the like. Once this object is achieved they lose interest in the Association until another opportunity arises for utilizing its force in the same way. Or if the

[17]Cf. Chapter V.

plea before the educational authorities is not successful, the principal may organize the Association for the purpose of raising the funds necessary to carry out the project. It is not that any aspect of this exploitation of the idea of an Association is necessarily vicious in any one case, but such emergency organizations, thrown together for quick action, inevitably raise up leaders and formulate policies which will militate against a constructive, permanent enterprise. It is a rare exception to find an organization which has come into existence only after careful explorations to discover the best type of leadership and considerable preliminary discussion to ensure the establishment of policies upon which alone a firm foundation for future achievement can be laid.

SCHOOL—PARENT-TEACHER ASSOCIATION RELATIONSHIPS

In the past the educational profession has generally assumed that, because the citizen was taxed to support the public education system, he exerted some kind of control over it. The assumption was valid enough in the days of the "little red schoolhouse" which was under the watchful surveillance of a small face-to-face community which completely comprehended the educational theory upon which the school operated. But to-day this assumption must be scrapped in practically every section of the United States, for the small community and the ready comprehension of educational policy are both rare in our industrialized form of society. Some provision must be made, however, for lay participation, if not control, in educational policy-making and in the educational process. One may remark, parenthetically, that it is an interesting fact that the citizens of a country founded on the principle that taxation without representation is tyranny have submitted for a long time to a situation in which their representation in regard to school matters has been entirely indirect. So far there has been no revolt on the part of the rank and file of citizens against the fact that education has been bureaucratically administered. Such revolts as have occurred have confined themselves to protests against modern educational theories and ideas which have created a serious situation, one which every conscientious modern educator who has faith in the new theories must wish to remedy. It constitutes the underlying reason why these educators are seeking to establish workable home-school relationships. One need only examine the many experimental methods evolved for substituting coöperation for ignorance and antagonism between these two institutions to be assured that a ferment is working to achieve a solution of the problem.

It is the contention in this thesis that the Parent-Teacher Association probably offers the most fruitful approach through which this coöperation can be brought about. The arguments are set forth in other parts of the study and need not be repeated here. But the real question which confronts educators is: Precisely what methods of administration can be adopted to deal with the Parent-Teacher Association in such a way that on the one hand the parents are admitted to legitimate participation in the educational process and on the other hand the school authorities are enabled to preserve their professional function and expert status? It is a problem not limited to the schools alone but broadly confronting our whole social order. Since it is fundamental in our society and since so little progress has been made with it (for appreciation even that the problem exists is limited to perhaps the last twenty years), it is possible in a study such as this only to make a few tentative suggestions as to how the problem might be solved and to hope that in the future an adequate solution will be made by many educators working together and reporting results.

On the basis of the material collected for this study, the author suggests the following to further the important work of the Parent-Teacher Association.

1. There should be general admission that a problem really exists. We who believe in modern educational theory should no longer be content with statements that coöperation cannot be achieved because neighborhood populations are shifting, because parents show no real interest, because foreign-language difficulties prevent exchange of views, because there are so many other activities taking up the time of parents, etc. These are all *conditions* to be met, not *reasons* for doing nothing about a real problem, and educators should stoutly maintain this point of view.

2. The conception that education is a social process must be developed and its implications acknowledged. One of these is that the schools must take the responsibility for training teachers who will view the school as an integral part of the larger social process which will result in a closer coöperation between the school and such a social agency as the Parent-Teacher Association. Such coöperation must be brought about if we would have the

home and the school accept their joint educational responsibilities. This involves re-orientation of the curriculum of most training schools in state colleges and universities. Community organization, sociology, social psychology, and anthropology must be emphasized in the courses of study during the preparatory period. (The pursuit of such studies, incidentally, would do much to infuse new vitality into the profession of teaching, which has for too many years recruited its ranks from persons who have had a narrow view of the responsibilities and possibilities of teaching, which on the whole most training institutions have done practically nothing to counteract.)

3. Educators must accept responsibility for keeping parents informed of what is going on in the school. This job cannot be done in the perfunctory and superficial way in which it has been carried on in the past if real coöperation is to be achieved between home and school. The responsibility of giving parents an accurate knowledge of administration and procedure presents a challenge to professional skill. The problem must be met in precisely the same spirit as that in which we are now working on methods of presenting subject matter in the school itself. In the end, it might involve actually adding another item to the list of attainments which are loosely grouped under professional prestige or proficiency. The ability to build up a sound understanding of the principles and methods followed in a particular school might conceivably have something to do with whether a teacher or principal was regarded as efficient by his colleagues and the profession at large. On the other side of the picture we might even see parents so informed regarding the wisdom of certain educational procedures that they will act as a corrective agency against exploitation of the schools by selfish interests. Since the educated person is the best parent, the school stands to gain from a program which keeps parents informed of school procedure.

4. In addition to taking responsibility for keeping parents informed as outlined above, the school must concern itself with parent education as such and must release money and leadership for that purpose. If the school does not take such responsibility this important body of new knowledge will not be disseminated on a scale vast enough to affect the behavior and attitudes of parents. No other institution in American life is equipped to make such information available to the rank and file of citizen-parents.

That this knowledge cannot be disseminated by a decree and that its inclusion in the responsibilities of the school involves the development of a new technique for adult education has been implied at a number of points in this thesis. The best present method seems to be the formation of small study groups under capable lay leadership, assisted by a corps of professional workers equipped with the requisite information. The interrelations between these lay and professional leaders must be clearly defined and it would seem from examining the experimental data available that the lay leadership will have to be given a scope and freedom of action which few adult organization leaders have thus far been accorded in the schools in those community efforts with which the schools have been associated—such as community centers, recreation centers, adult night schools, and the like.

In regard to this form of joint parent-and-school responsibility, it would also seem valid to suggest that the enterprise be at least partly, if not wholly, self-supporting, that is, that the parents contribute the major part of the sums needed. This could be arranged either by adoption of the "pay-as-you-go" policy so well developed theoretically[18] a few years ago by the groups interested in the wider use of the school; or by building on the practice now common in the Parent-Teacher Association of subsidizing certain school activities, for example, buying equipment, giving charity, setting up scholarships, etc. The practice would be the same, but the money would in this instance be utilized for the education of parents instead of for the support of activities which should properly be taken care of by the tax-budget if our theory of free education for the child means anything. This is not the place to argue the fine points of community organization theory, but the wider implication of the financial problems involved is stated here merely to indicate the really profound ramifications involved in the apparently simple suggestion that the schools should take the responsibility for parent education.

5. Still another step must be taken by the school. It must evolve some administrative set-up for dealing with the Parent-Teacher Association which will enable the latter to contribute toward the formation of sound educational policies and to coöperate effectively and creatively on school projects and activities so that

[18]See "Proceedings of the National Community Center Associations," in the *Annual Reports* of the N.E.A. from 1918 to 1930.

both the parents and the school will benefit. This involves, on the part of the school, formal recognition of the Association, of its function, and of its potentialities. What contribution it will make and what forms its coöperation will take depend to a great extent on the personalities of the members of the school faculty and of the lay leaders of the Association and they will undoubtedly vary in each school. But the suggestion here made is that a method be worked out which will give formal recognition to the Association in each school. Based on the experimental data available, the author makes the suggestion that this formal relationship can best be expressed by the formation of an executive committee within the Association on which the principal or designated teachers may sit as *ex-officio* members.

The status of *ex-officio* is suggested because it best indicates that kind of *advisory* relation with the Association which is all the principal and teachers should have. To assume any office in the Association would naturally place the faculty in the position of controlling Association policy, because of the power which it can exert as the highest school authority and which, being human, it could not fail to exert if given the opportunity. The practice prevalent in many Associations to-day of giving the principal virtual *veto* power over the plans of the organization is bad, for able parents will not be drawn into an Association which functions as a spineless adjunct of the principal's office.

To fill adequately the rôle of advisor and expert in the Association requires considerable skill and, fundamentally, belief on the part of the principal in the efficacy of community organization. He must be willing to have his policies questioned, his theories subjected to analysis, his school procedure open to suggestions for improvements and changes. It involves him in the difficult situation of pleasing two masters, his lay public and his professional superiors. Nothing except a recognition that such *is* actually his situation, whether he recognizes it or not, in the American educational philosophy, will support him in the annoyances and irritations and challenges to his professional pride which such a procedure entails. But the results are well worth the effort. He will be assisting in the development of community leaders; he will be able to iron out the latent antagonisms which frustrate so much of his best professional work; he will gain support for the development and extension of his school plant; he will be able in the long run to do a professional job which will be a source of legitimate pride to himself and undoubtedly increase his prestige among his colleagues. There are sound gains to be made both for the community in which he works and for his own personal interests by experimenting with this administrative relationship with the Parent-Teacher Association.

It is interesting to note that many of the important suggestions which have furthered educational progress in this country have been made by the laity; and such a relationship as is here suggested seems to hold the promise of increasing and strengthening the contribution of the laity to educational experiments and departures in which direction it already has an honorable record. Much of our school work is so unsatisfactory that it seems short-sighted to overlook any source which might contribute toward its improvement and toward the realization of more permanent achievement.

6. But this formal recognition which can be given voluntarily by the principal and teachers is, in the opinion of the author, not enough to insure the necessary prestige and standing of the Associations. Their powers and status should be recognized in the by-laws of the boards of education in each city. This will enable them to speak with authority on budget matters and the lay administration of the schools. The present legal machinery for administering the school system is lodged with a small number of people elected at large or appointed by some municipal head, known as the board of education. Without exception these are lay persons and they are supposed to represent the citizen power over education. But how many of them are trained to wield such power in the best interests of the school? How often are they not subservient to the political interests which appointed them? How much of the red tape, confusion, and muddled policies of many educational systems is due to this conflict of interests to which the legal authority in the educational system is subjected? If we are to eradicate this system, which seems grounded in American institutions, we must find some way of building up a so-called "pressure group"—to use the language of the political scientists; this will help to check the political exploitation of the schools and will do so in no antagonistic, critical, negative spirit, but by substituting a program of well-thought-out, sound educa-

tional ideas for which it is willing to fight. In the past, such pressure groups as have been formed have represented only a minute fraction of our population, mostly the well-to-do who had only a theoretical interest in public education; and these groups have not indeed been representative at all of the rank and file of parents, who, in the last analysis, are those citizens with the most profound stake in our public education system. That boards of education will voluntarily offer the necessary recognition to Parent-Teacher Associations is unlikely. The Associations will have to insist on such recognition and it will be to the best interests of the professional educator to support their efforts in this direction. The patient educational work which the individual schools would perform under the scheme here outlined would prepare leaders among the parents to fill the rôle of city-wide leadership, equipped with sound knowledge of the schools and their problems and with workable and creative suggestions for meeting them.

7. In conclusion, the author suggests that aside from these administrative and extra-legal devices, the most important consideration in the development of a sound working relationship between the school and the home is the *attitude* of the principal and his faculty. Any administrative procedure can be made to function autocratically and arbitrarily, or the reverse. It all depends on the individual in power since no safeguards ever invented can prevent an individual in authority from using power selfishly, or autocratically. This is especially true when the individual in question is fortified by expert knowledge and is dealing with a loosely-formed organization made up of people relatively ignorant of his specialty and oppressed with personal problems which they have never been equipped to deal with in abstract terms and in relation to a larger perspective. It is so easy, with the multitudinous duties thrust upon the principal of a modern school, to dismiss the queries of such groups, queries usually couched in non-academic terms, ill-expressed, perhaps only half-articulated. It is so easy to carry over the attitude with which an elder person deals with children, to his dealings with adults. To reverse this process, to be patient with stumbling and meagre intellectual processes while at the same time treating the person as an adult of equal standing, makes large demands upon the administrator and the person clothed with authority. The

inspiring results which conceivably might flow from such effort, both in personal development and in the rise of a new kind of integrated community around the local schoolhouse, with the fruitful influences it might have on education generally, seem to be quite enough to justify accepting the challenge involved in these new concepts. The strength to support such attitudes will be found in the allegiance of the individual principal to the principles of democracy as conceived in the United States, as well as in his devotion to the right of individual self-development which is theoretically guaranteed to every American citizen. Why should our educational institutions shut off the opportunity for such self-development to adults who are not enrolled as students in the schools? Why not make these Parent-Teacher Associations a field for the development of community leaders and a means of widening the horizons of the rank and file? Once embarked on the experiment of sincere adherence to the attitude suggested here, it is the author's conclusion, from the observations made, that the satisfaction of watching the development of individual parents who respond to such an attitude will be quite enough to stimulate further effort, to say nothing of the actual practical results in smoother working of the school administration which inevitably follow.

The following specific functions indicate the mutual interdependence of the school and the Parent-Teacher Association and show definitely the work of the school and the Parent-Teacher Association with reference to important functions which concern both groups. These functions should be considered by no means all-inclusive.

THE WORK OF THE SCHOOL AND THE PARENT-TEACHER
ASSOCIATION WITH REFERENCE TO IMPORTANT
FUNCTIONS CONCERNING BOTH GROUPS

PHILOSOPHY OF EDUCATION

School	Parent-Teacher Association
A philosophy of education should be formulated by the school which will provide an inclusive program of education. Parents' aid should be sought through discussions and conferences.	The schools need the parent's aid and point of view to establish a stable philosophy. Therefore the Parent-Teacher Association should assist in formulating an educational philosophy.

CURRICULUM AND METHOD

School	Parent-Teacher Association
The Parent-Teacher Association should be consulted to bring to light the practical aspect of the work and problems peculiar to the community. No course should be set up without considering the views and opinions of a lay public.	One of the objectives of the Parent-Teacher Association should be to keep informed regarding the content and procedure of the school work.

TEACHER EFFICIENCY

The school, because it is qualified by training to judge the work and efficiency of the teacher, should have this responsibility.	The reaction of the parent to the work of the teacher is helpful to school administration. An intelligent discussion of the teacher's work and problems by parent and teacher is desirable.

TEACHER TRAINING

Accepted standards should be required by the school administration.	Parent influence can demand that salaries be sufficient to command fit and adequate standards.

PARENT EDUCATION

The school should assist in formulating a plan of Parent Education. It should furnish leadership, propose methods, and assist in selection of subject matter. Such a plan should be financed partly by the Board of Education.	Parents should be responsible for organizing groups for instruction. They should select leaders and subject matter; classify interests of parents; and support a plan to make the school system responsible for releasing money for Parent Education. Parent Education should be the important part of a Parent Teacher Association program.

SCHOOL PROBLEMS

This is the responsibility of the school administration, but the co-operation of parents should be sought to acquire needed data and information about the child.	The Parent-Teacher Association should give the school information about the child such as pupil history, background, special interests. The views of the Parent-Teacher Association regarding the success or failure of the school are helpful.

School

Parent-Teacher Association

The school needs to study community problems and to keep the community informed about its educational program. The Parent-Teacher Association and other parent groups are a valuable medium. The school cannot do its work without the support of the tax-paying public.

The study of local conditions should be the joint project of the school and the Parent-Teacher Association. Community groups should work with and for the schools. An extensive publicity program is imperative.

CHILD PSYCHOLOGY

The school should be delegated to acquire as much information about the child as possible.

The Parent-Teacher Association needs to keep informed regarding the psychology of the child and of learning. The program of the Association should include much on this subject. Opportunities to study child psychology should be sought by the Parent-Teacher Association. Leaders should be secured in and out of the school system to direct classes in child psychology.

SCHOOL EQUIPMENT

The board of education is responsible for the provision of suitable educational equipment.

The Parent-Teacher Association should not assume responsibility of the board with reference to the purchasing of school equipment. Where the school suffers because of faulty administration, the buying of equipment by the Parent-Teacher Association is a proper activity provided it does not interfere with the educational program.

SUMMARY

This study of the form and technique of organization of the Parent-Teacher Association and its relation to the school, based on a consideration of its purpose and function and a survey of practices in the National Congress and in one hundred local units, seems to yield the following conclusions:

1. It is advisable in the organization of local units that the original impetus proceed from the parents themselves, although the

school may indirectly suggest the need and influence the formation of an organization.

2. National and state organizations of Parent-Teacher Associations or, in the case of independent units, responsible centralized authority, should provide more skillful leadership and assistance to local Associations in matters of organization technique. This assistance should include a recognition of the fact that each community has specific local needs and should, in addition, embrace helpful suggestions in regard to such matters as the type of leadership required for success, program, publicity, community organization, conduct of meetings, school and home relationship, community articulation, and so forth.

3. The number of activities suggested by the National Congress should be reduced to allow each local unit to plan a program based on specific needs.

4. Local Associations should be admitted to the State and National Congresses only when their programs are based on accepted standards and meet requirements approved by these two bodies.

5. These requirements should include a definite recognition of the fact that the major function of the Parent-Teacher Association is parent education. The program, therefore, should include a majority of activities which are educational and which provide for local needs.

6. Emphasis should be placed on developing an interest on the part of men, both parents and teachers, in the work of the Parent-Teacher Association.

7. There is great variation in the number of meetings held by the different Associations. Meetings should be held at least once a month at convenient times and places. Since more frequent meetings are advisable to solve specific problems or further the continuity of the program, provision should be made for them.

8. A concerted effort should be made to gain extra-legal recognition of the Parent-Teacher Association from the boards of education. This effort could well be stimulated by the National Congress and would do much to increase the prestige and stability of local Associations.

9. Factors most important in the development of a sound working relationship between the school and Parent-Teacher Association are:

a) Admission of existing problem.

b) Conception of education as a social process.

c) Responsibility on the part of educators for keeping parents informed of what is going on in school.

d) A parent education plan on the part of the school.

e) Recognition of the Parent-Teacher Association in the by-laws of the board of education.

f) Attitude of principal and his staff toward the home.

g) Definition of specific functions.

CHAPTER IV

PUBLICITY AND FINANCE IN PARENT-TEACHER ASSOCIATIONS

PUBLICITY

COMMERCIAL enterprises have long recognized the fact that publicity is a necessity in order to secure acceptance of their ideas on the part of the public. This is true not only of commercial enterprises. It is equally true of any modern community organization which wishes to acquire public prestige and confidence. Increasingly this fact is being accepted by the leaders in Parent-Teacher Association work. A great many competent judges now believe that in order to forward a constructive educational program for parents it is necessary to include as a major activity in association work an effective publicity set-up.[1] Table C[2] indicates also the important position publicity now occupies in the estimation of State Presidents of the Parent-Teacher Association.

In general, however, the principles, aims, and methods of publicity have not been clearly understood and for this reason the publicity activity of the Parent-Teacher Association has been less than satisfactory. Indeed, it has been limited, uninteresting, and unsuccessful.

Considering newspaper publicity alone, the writer found that editors in fifteen cities ranked Parent-Teacher Association news from fair to poor. Nearly all the editors claim that Parent-Teacher Associations do not submit interesting reports of their activities. In addition, the presentation of the news of their activities is often poor. All the editors felt that they would publish more Parent-Teacher Association news if it were more interesting in content and in preparation. Farley,[3] listing thirteen school items used by the press, showed that Parent-Teacher Association news ranked thirteenth in quantity used in school re-

[1]Cf. Chapter IV, Table 2.
[2]See Appendix, Table C.
[3]Farley, Belmont. *What to Tell the People About the Public Schools.* Bureau of Publications, Teachers College, Columbia University, New York City, 1929. Page 37.

40

ports. He also showed, in a study of 101 weeklies and 15 dailies, that Athletics had a score of 88 as compared with a score of 45 for Parent-Teacher Association news.

In ranking thirteen school topics in order of interest, 5,067 school patrons gave the news of Parent-Teacher Association activities a mean rank of twelve. Only two cities of the thirteen considered in the survey gave Parent-Teacher Association news a rank as high as ten. The other eleven cities ranked it twelve or thirteen. Thirty-nine boards of education scattered throughout the United States also gave reports of Parent-Teacher Association activities the lowest rank in interest out of a group of thirteen school activities.

Reynolds[4] found that in 98 cities a large majority of editors rated the potential value of Parent-Teacher Association news as very high. Only 24 per cent of the editors print Parent-Teacher Association news daily. In the 98 cities included in his survey, he found:

24% published Parent-Teacher Association news *daily.*
22% published Parent-Teacher Association news *irregularly.*
6% published Parent-Teacher Association news *unspecified times.*
3% published Parent-Teacher Association news *weekly.*
2% published Parent-Teacher Association news *monthly.*
2% published Parent-Teacher Association news *not at all.*
41% did not answer.

Most of the above material is, of course, concerned only with the press publicity of the Parent-Teacher Association. It is indicative, however, of the general weakness of the Association's present publicity activity.

There are many avenues of publicity open to the Parent-Teacher Association. Among these we may list: word of mouth, specialized publications, daily and weekly newspapers, handbills, and posters. All these means may be utilized in acquainting the public with the functions and purposes of the Association. But in the use of any of these avenues, the indispensable element is "news value." Something has to be about to happen, or must have happened, in order to secure any kind of publicity. The thing that has happened or is about to happen must be interesting in itself and must be interestingly presented or any attempts at arousing public interest through publicity will fail.

[4]Reynolds, Rollo G. *Newspaper Publicity for the Public Schools.* A. G. Seiler, 1224 Amsterdam Ave., New York City, 1922. Page 39.

Among the activities engaging the attention of the Parent-Teacher Associations which have a definite news value, we may list:

1. Programs including addresses by distinguished speakers.
2. Entertainments and special nights for parents and visitors.
3. Parties and receptions.
4. A membership campaign.
5. Lectures of Parent-Teacher Association officials before other civic groups.
6. Joint projects with other civic groups.
7. Projects undertaken by the Parent-Teacher Association.
8. Projects for community betterment.

These activities, though they may in some cases be in themselves unimportant, would serve the purpose of bringing the attention of the public to the work of the Parent-Teacher Association. After this has been done a more specific expression of the duties and functions of the Parent-Teacher Association would be possible.

The first step in a publicity program is the creation of items of news value. The second step is the presentation of these items to the public through the avenues of publicity listed above and by means of the following devices:

1. Printed programs.
2. Exhibition of scrapbook showing activities.
3. Telephone.
4. Radio.
5. Theatre.
6. Bulletin board.
7. Convention reports.
8. Library.
9. Superintendent's Annual Report to the Board of Education.
10. School papers.

Although all these avenues, devices, and items of news interest are at present used by the Parent-Teacher Association, they are unfortunately not used to their best advantage, as is exemplified by the study of newspaper publicity of the Parent-Teacher Association at the beginning of the chapter. One reason for this failure, the lack of knowledge of methods of publicity, has already been listed. A further reason for this failure is that in many cases the people in charge of publicity are not always entirely clear about the policies, functions, purposes, and plans of their Association and are likely to fall into the error of looking upon publicity work as an end in itself, or as a means of increasing membership solely, instead of considering it as a means of increasing the prestige of the organization and bringing the public to an understanding of its civic importance.

FINANCE

Turning now to a consideration of the finances of the Parent-Teacher Association, we may note that local units have always been self-supporting. Any study of this situation is valuable only to the extent that it correlates an understanding of the character and sources of income and expenditure with a realization of the part that income and expenditure play in directing and influencing the activity of the group.

The basis of income for most local community organizations is the membership fee, although in some organizations membership is free. The fees range from twenty-five cents a term to one dollar per year. In many Associations one dollar is the charge for family rather than for individual membership. Supplementing this source of income in the local Association, money may be raised through such means as entertainments, sales, advertising, donations, card parties, and gifts. The majority of the Associations feel that it is necessary to supplement the tax budget in order to provide money for school equipment, charity and relief.[5] This feeling was encouraged originally in order to direct the activity of the Parent-Teacher Associations into channels that would interfere little with the educational prerogatives and ideas of the school system. It has grown to such an unfortunate extent, however, that the budgets of most Associations do not include any item to care for the important work of parent education. At present, however, there is an improvement in attitude to be noted[6] and some organizations are beginning to recognize their neglect of this most important function. A few organizations have planned for parent education as an item of cost in their budgets.

Where a program of parent education has been adopted, it is usually financed with funds provided by members and by means of volunteer or trained leadership not attached to the local school faculties. A very few cities have taken over the responsibility of

[5]Associations of high rank raise funds in a dignified way, using one concerted effort to secure needed money.

[6]Particularly in New York, California and other states where Parent Education agencies have carried on considerable propaganda.

parent education, assuming at the same time all financial obligations. But such a scheme is necessarily a part of the school program and is controlled by the school.

In 1924 Butterworth[7] found that an undue emphasis was placed on the money-raising activities of local Associations. In nine states 50.3 per cent of the activities performed by 598 Associations in communities with a population of 2,500 or less were activities to provide money for the school. For communities above 2,500 population the average percentage of money raising activities was 41.1 per cent.

Table D[8] shows the activities entered upon by one hundred Associations, selected at random throughout the United States, for the purpose of raising money. The methods are arranged in order of frequency.

Table F[9] shows how these one hundred Associations spent their money.

That the various Parent-Teacher Associations have had financial struggles is unfortunate, but the policy of self-support has many advantages. It may in some respects be difficult but it protects the Associations from outside control. It also affords them a greater opportunity to influence policies, legislation, and educational practice. Rogers[10] says, "If parents are not independent of the school the civic potentialities of the movement must in a large measure be abandoned at the beginning."

Assuming, therefore, that self-support is desirable, it would seem that after a policy of self-support is undertaken it would then be advisable for the educational authorities to place at the disposal of the Association some financial resources and leadership in its personnel. Writing on this point, Rogers[11] says:

If the plan of self-support is adopted immediate problems are presented. The first is the kind of relationship which can be worked out between the parent organization and the educational authorities. There is no doubt that the educational system should assist the movement in some way because its own efficiency stands to gain by the coöperation of educated parents. It would seem that the most logical plan is for the educational authorities to make available to the parent organization assistance on the technical aspects

[7]Butterworth, J. E. *Op. cit.*
[8]See Appendix, Table D.
[9]See Appendix, Table F.
[10]Rogers, M. L. *A Contribution to the Theory and Practice of Parent-Teacher Associations in the United States.* United Parents Associations, New York City, 1931. Page 68.
[11]Rogers, M. L. *Op. cit.*

of study group work, while leaving the parents free to initiate and pursue the other activities here suggested as highly important. Such a plan is now in operation in New York State and working admirably.

Let us now consider the income and expenditures of the National Congress which is largely supported by the dues of the members of the local Congress units. As a rule, fifteen cents of the membership fee of each individual member of each local Association is sent to the State Congress, which retains ten cents for its own budget and forwards five cents to the National Congress. The total receipts of the National Congress from forty-eight Associations for the year 1930–1931 were $93,581.19.[12] To this total must be added further receipts of $23,773.40 collected by the Congress office. This includes the return from publications, emblems, conventions, interest, returns from the field, and other miscellaneous items.

Founders' Day, established to celebrate the birthday of the Congress, provided considerable revenue in the form of gifts from local units through state organizations. One-half of the sum raised in a state on Founders' Day is kept in the state for extension purposes. The other half is sent to the national treasurer by the state treasurer.

More specific information as to the proportional distribution of income according to source is shown in Table E.[13] Similarly, the distribution of the expenditure of the national organization is shown in Table G.[14] We may note, generally, that the total expenditure was $116,089.54, over 34 per cent of which or $40,000 was spent for salaries. No national officer receives a salary. However, the national office and directors of departments spent $12,663.09. An item of $3,554.14 represents money expended for conducting the campaign to correct the physical defects of children entering school for the first time, known as the "Summer Round-Up,"[15] and an item of $7,902.47 provides for the expenses incurred by secretaries for work done in the field.

The State Congress income, comprising a fee of ten cents per member in most states, is usually expended for such general ex-

[12]A statement of receipts of the National Congress for this year may be obtained from 1201 16th Street N. W., Washington, D. C.

[13]See Appendix, Table E.

[14]See Appendix, Table G.

[15]Reeve, M. W. and Lombard, E. C. *The Parent-Teacher Association, 1924–1926,* U. S. Bulletin 1927, No. 11. Page 9.

penses as conventions, travel, office expenses, bulletins, and publicity.

SUMMARY

The study of the publicity activities and the financial system of the Parent-Teacher Association makes it possible to set up the following recommendations.

Publicity

Since publicity is considered an item of major importance by many judges of the Parent-Teacher Association activities, and since the present publicity activity of the organization is demonstrably insufficient, it should therefore be the subject of more careful consideration than has been given to it in the past. In doing this, however, care should be taken that the Associations do not fall into the opposite error of placing too much emphasis upon publicity. It is valuable only as a *means*. With these things in mind, therefore, the following recommendations are presented:

1. Parent-Teacher Association officials must understand clearly the purposes, plans, functions, and policies of their organization in order to administer an effective publicity department.

2. Since publicity is classified under three headings, (a) the creation of items of news value, (b) avenues and (c) devices to be used, each one of these should be subjected to separate study in order to see how their usefulness may be increased, and the three studies should then be coördinated into a working publicity program which should comprise the following items:

a) The Parent-Teacher Association should be dynamic and aggressive in making its activities interesting enough to appeal to the press.

b) Methods employed by publicity experts should be studied and applied to the needs of Parent-Teacher Association work.

c) Training for publicity work should be made available and required of all state workers in charge of the publicity work of the Parent-Teacher Association.

d) There should be an organized publicity set-up under the direction of a competent chairman who should receive help from a trained expert provided by the State and National

Congress[16] or from some high centralized authority on association work. This help should include a set of principles governing the selection, organization, style, and composition of materials as well as a system of submitting news in a manner satisfactory to the local editor.

3. News should be collected and released systematically before and after all meetings, including annual group meetings. This should be supplemented with news and plans of the Association as formulated by the president and the executive committee.

4. Cordial relations must be established between the Parent-Teacher Association and the press.

5. The 49 Congress Units which considered publicity important enough to give it third place in order of frequency in a list of 61 activities mentioned in their reports[17] to the National Congress, should encourage the local units to make more use of a constructive publicity program. (See Appendix, Table C).

6. The state publicity program should be placed on a business basis with a definite budget administered under the direction of the president.

Finance

1. There should be definite dues for membership.

2. The Parent-Teacher Association should be financially independent if it is to have an effective influence in the community. The local school system may then provide some aid since it must recognize that the work of the Parent-Teacher Association will result in an increase in the efficiency of its educational work. An enlightened parent will be of inestimable value to child, school, and community.

3. Finally, in budgeting the expense of local units it must be continually borne in mind that the Association's major work is to be parent education, and money and interest should not be expended beyond a point where such expenditure threatens to interfere with a well-rounded educational program.

[16]In 1929, 149 students took correspondence courses offered by the National Congress of Parents and Teachers. *Proceedings* of the National Congress of Parents and Teachers, 1929. Page 91. [17]*Ibid.* Pages 30–31.

CHAPTER V

FUNCTIONS, PURPOSES, AND ACTIVITIES OF THE PARENT-TEACHER ASSOCIATION

THE purpose of this chapter is to compare the theoretical functions and purposes of the Parent-Teacher Association with the activities in which the separate Associations are engaged, and to attempt to discover what relation exists between the two. In a perfectly adjusted organization we would find that all the activities of the group were directed toward a successful achievement of its theoretical purposes. In the attempt to discover how nearly true this is of the work of the Parent-Teacher Association, three distinct studies were made.

The first is an evaluation by forty directing officers of the Parent-Teacher Association and forty administrators in the field of education, of sixteen primary purposes and functions of the Parent-Teacher Association. The result of this study indicates what, in the opinions of the leaders of the work, should be the objectives toward which the Association should work. Their opinions represent a theoretical approach to the subject.

The second study is an evaluation by one hundred presidents of local Parent-Teacher Associations and one hundred school administrators, such as principals of schools and supervisors, of the most important activities which in their opinion should occupy the attention of local Parent-Teacher Associations. The jurors in this study represent a group that is in more direct and intimate contact with the practical work in the field. They have a realization and an understanding of the theoretical approach exemplified in the first study, but the limitations imposed by practical activity impinge upon them more immediately than upon the first group.

The third study is a compilation of the activities actually carried on by one hundred Parent-Teacher Associations studied by the author.

STUDY ONE

The theoretical functions and purposes of the Parent-Teacher Association were selected from a careful analysis of literature on the

48

subject and from a study of books written in the field. This analysis was supplemented by a study of state and national reports, proceedings, programs, annual meetings, and constitutions. Combining the results from these two sources, sixteen objectives toward which the work of the Parent-Teacher Association is supposedly directed were selected and presented to forty Parent-Teacher Association officials for purposes of ranking them in the order of their importance.[1] These officials were selected from the roster of administrative officers of national or state federations or paid experts employed by the National Congress, and from officers and experts of independent state and city federations as well. These officers gave their judgments and the scale was then submitted to forty administrators in the field of education. Many of these were students of Administration and Elementary Education at Teachers College, Columbia University, capable of giving an intelligent and unbiased report.

In summarizing the opinions of these two groups, the following technique was used: The rank given an objective by the individual juror was considered the score for that objective. The total sum of such scores for a single objective would be the final score of each objective, as shown in Table 1. A low total score indicates a more important objective, since a rating of 1 to 16 in order of importance was given by each juror. The lowest possible score in point of importance is, therefore, 640. The highest possible score is 40.

In summarizing the results of the above judgments we find that there is some agreement about the comparative importance of the functions and purposes as ranked by the two groups. Thus, although the Parent-Teacher Association officials would rank *Child development* first and *The parents' rôle in modern education* second, and the educational administrators reverse this judgment, nevertheless both groups assign to both activities places of the highest importance. The greatest difference in opinion is found in regard to *Coöperation in solving school problems*. The administrator would evidently reserve this function for the schools.

On other matters, however, the correlation between the two groups is significant. These judges show a strong tendency to pull away from non-educational activities and to devote the attention of the Associations to activities designed to educate the parent

[1]See Appendix for scale of rating social values of theoretical objectives of Parents Associations or Parent-Teacher Associations, pages 119–120.

TABLE 1

IMPORTANT OBJECTIVES OF PARENT-TEACHER ASSOCIATION AS RANKED BY
40 ASSOCIATION PRESIDENTS AND 40 SCHOOL ADMINISTRATORS

OBJECTIVE	PRESIDENTS' RANKING		ADMINISTRA-TORS' RANKING	
	Rank	Score	Rank	Score
Providing information to bring about changes for the better in regard to *child development*, habits of learning, etc............................	1	193	2	192
Providing an understanding of the *parents' rôle in modern education*, the value and opportunities of the Parent-Teacher Association, etc...........	2	198	1	163
Coöperating with the educational staff to solve *school problems* such as homework, reading habits, etc..	3	217	7	273
Providing a means for *social intercourse* between parents and teachers, etc.....................	4	230	4	236
Organizing and assisting *study groups in child development*, the parent-child relationship generally known as "parent education"................	5	237	3	233
Helping toward a better understanding of *community conditions*, needs, etc.....................	6	286	6	264
Working to correct *physical defects* of children through such devices as the "Summer Round-Up," etc...................................	7	301	10	358
Providing general knowledge of the *school philosophy*, curriculum-making in relation to the changing social situation, etc......................	8	304	8	280
Working on a legislative program for better school conditions, etc.............................	9	329	5	240
Supporting state national organizations in their efforts for *equalization of educational opportunities*, etc.......................................	10	358	9	328
Providing *charitable relief* for families of poor in the school district, etc...........................	11	381	14	434
Educating the public as to the Association's program, *publicity set-up*, etc.....................	12	420	13	379
Financing *experimental work in the school curriculum* to be used as demonstrators, etc..............	13	423	12	377
Providing scholarships for gifted children........	14	476	11	367
Making material gifts to the school such as pictures, radios, various kinds of equipment, not provided by the school board.........................	15	504	16	488
Providing a *cultural program* with no necessary emphasis on the needs of the child, etc.........	16	514	15	452

Note: A low rank or score indicates an objective of primary importance.

and to help the child. Thus, cultural activities with no necessary emphasis on the needs of the child and the making of material gifts to the school are given the last two places by both groups while more direct educational activities are rated higher.

The above, then, is the attitude of a number of leaders in Parent-Teacher Association work and leaders in educational thought. The judgments on the scale are admittedly incomplete but they do provide us with an understanding of a point of view. We can see from a study of their scales what, in the opinions of these judges, are the significant functions and purposes of the Parent-Teacher Association.

STUDY TWO

Let us turn now to a consideration of the activities which, in the opinion of those Parent-Teacher Association officials and school administrators in more direct contact with the work in the field, are considered of primary importance.

After a careful study of the work and program of one hundred Associations, supplemented by an analysis of national and state proceedings and reports as well as an examination of programs, meetings, resolutions, periodicals, and opinions of administrators, eleven activities occurring most frequently as major activities in the program of the Parent-Teacher Association were listed and included in a questionnaire.[2] This questionnaire was sent to one hundred presidents of local Parent-Teacher Associations and to one hundred school administrators (principals, and so forth).[3] They were asked to evaluate in terms of importance the eleven activities listed.

Table 2 is a summary of their judgments. A technique similar to that used in scoring the judgments on Parent-Teacher Association proposed functions and purposes was used. The rank given an activity by the juror was considered the score of that activity. The total sum of such scores as given by the one hundred jurors would be the final score of each activity as shown in Table 2. Since each activity was numbered 1 to 11 in order of importance by each juror, a low numerical score would indicate the more important activity. The lowest possible score in point of importance is, therefore, 1,100. The highest possible score is 100.

A consideration of Table 2 reveals a perfect correlation in the judgments of the two sets of jurors on Activities Nos. 1, 3, 4, and

[2] See Appendix, page 125.

[3] See Appendix, page 125, for list of coöperating states.

10.   Also both groups give *Entertainments* and *Making of gifts to the school* a low rating, although the school administrators, again apparently zealous to defend their administrative prerogatives, place *Solving of certain school problems* in last place as contrasted with the eighth place given this activity by the Parent-Teacher Association presidents.

TABLE 2

IMPORTANT ACTIVITIES AS RANKED BY 100 ASSOCIATION PRESIDENTS AND
100 SCHOOL ADMINISTRATORS

ACTIVITY	PRESIDENTS' RANKING		ADMINISTRATORS' RANKING	
	Rank	Score	Rank	Score
Study Groups*..............................	1	273	1	308
Program of Parent Education..................	2	341	5	457
Study of Child Psychology....................	3	346	3	424
Study of School Work and Methods.............	4	436	4	431
Community Projects...........................	5	561	2	419
Demonstrations or Exhibits of School Problems...	6	567	6	472
Publicity....................................	7	603	8	527
Solving Certain School Problems...............	8	647	11	777
Social Intercourse...........................	9	698	7	500
Entertainments..............................	10	846	10	724
Making Gifts to School.......................	11	859	9	676

Note: A low score or rank indicates an activity of primary importance.
*See Appendix for definition and detailed explanation of study groups.   Pages 117-118.

In this set of judgments also we find a tendency to pull away from non-educational activities and to direct the interests and energies of the group toward a study of the child, of education, and of parenthood.   This tendency is not so marked as it was in the first study, a fact which can be accounted for by the difference in points of view of the judges.   Therefore, we find that whereas in the first study *Parent education* was given third place in order of importance by the administrators, it is given only fifth place in the second study by the administrators.

There is demonstrated, therefore, a slight lag in the attitude of the administrators in the field behind that of the judges with a more purely theoretical approach, further removed from the field problems.

STUDY THREE

Let us turn finally to a consideration of the activities which are actually being carried on by the Parent-Teacher Association.   One hundred Parent-Teacher Associations were studied and a table compiled indicating the activities in which these one hundred Associations engaged. The meetings of the Associations at which these activities originate or take place, occur on the average of nine times a year.[4] The meetings usually begin at 8:15

TABLE 3–A

ACTIVITIES CARRIED ON BY 100 PARENT-TEACHER ASSOCIATIONS IN ORDER
OF FREQUENCY

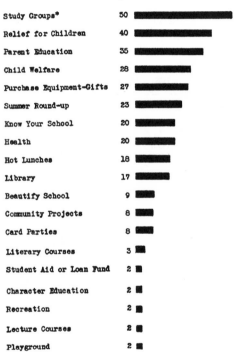

Study Groups*	50
Relief for Children	40
Parent Education	35
Child Welfare	28
Purchase Equipment-Gifts	27
Summer Round-up	23
Know Your School	20
Health	20
Hot Lunches	18
Library	17
Beautify School	9
Community Projects	8
Card Parties	8
Literary Courses	3
Student Aid or Loan Fund	2
Character Education	2
Recreation	2
Lecture Courses	2
Playground	2

*Includes variety of subjects such as: Education of the Child, Parent and Child, Child Relationships, School Work and Methods, etc.

and last from one hour and a half to two hours, not including the time spent in social intercourse. These regular association meetings are not to be confused with the meetings of committees, study groups, council or state meetings.

[4]Compare Chapter II, page 25.

A typical agenda[5] follows:

1. Opening, singing, minutes, etc.
2. Business session, reports, committees, announcements by the President, etc.
3. Entertainment.
4. Topic for the evening, lectures, discussion, demonstration.
5. Plans for the next meeting.
6. Social hour.

Considering this agenda, it would seem possible under Items 2, 4 and 5 to achieve a great deal of activity which would be in line with the theoretical purposes and functions of the group. However, a consideration of Tables 3–A and 3–B will indicate to what

TABLE 3–B

ACTIVITIES MENTIONED ONCE ONLY

Raising Money	Art
Music Appreciation	Adult Reading Program
Humane Education	Festivals
Correlation of Home and School	Distribution of Clothing
Educational Program	Fathers' Night
Free Milk	Minstrel Show
Scouting	Operetta
Nutrition	Social Welfare
Social	Child's Reading
First Aid	Vocational Guidance
Parliamentary Work	Pageantry
Preschool Examination	Banquets
Courtesy Drives	Oratory
Mother Choruses	Class Demonstrations
School Museum	Disease Prevention
Better Films	Social Times for Parents and Teachers
Cafeteria	Radio Lectures
Use of Leisure Time	Better Parks
Safety Traffic	Promoting Friendliness and Good Will
Clinics	Motion Pictures
Mother Singers	Rummage Sales
Theatricals and Dramatics	Red Cross
Mental Hygiene	

extent the activities of the group are dispersed and the general diffusion of interest found in the field. While all the important activities are represented in the listing, there is an almost overwhelming inclusion of activities which are neither valuable nor directed.

[5]One hundred programs representing Associations throughout the United States.

When we examine these activities in the light of the proposed functions and purposes considered as important—in the light even of the activities considered as important by the two sets of judges in Studies One and Two—there is seen to be a great discrepancy between function and activity. It is significant that, although the judges in both studies relegated the *Making of gifts to the school* to a very low place, it nevertheless, in the activities actually engaging the attention of the group, occupies one of the highest places. In addition we find listed such extraneous matters as *Beautify school, Relief for children, Community projects, Card parties*, and the other activities on Table 3–B listed as mentioned only once. These are all activities which, though in themselves they may be a very essential part of the people's lives, nevertheless bear little or no relation to the functions and purposes of the Parent-Teacher Association. While it may be argued that in themselves they do little harm, it is important to consider that they take time away from the more important activities which should be engrossing the attention of the group, and in this way they weaken the efficiency and civic significance of the Association.

SUMMARY AND CONCLUSIONS

Comparing the results of the three studies made in this chapter, there is seen to be a clear understanding and agreement on the part of Parent-Teacher Association officials and educational authorities in regard to the functions of the Parent-Teacher Association. There is, however, a slight discrepancy between the functions considered important by this group and the activities considered important by the group of judges in closer contact with the work in the field. And there is a much greater discrepancy between the ideas of either of these two groups and the actual work being carried on by the local Parent-Teacher Associations.

If the Association is to continue its work and become an association with definite significance in the field of education and child welfare, there must be a closer coördination between the theoretical statement of functions and purposes and the activity of the Association. The purposes and functions of the Association, as understood by the people who are at the head of the work, must also be clearly understood by the local Associations and all their activities must be directed toward the furtherance of their defined purposes.

With this in mind, therefore, Chapter VII is offered as a specific recommendation of one method by which the activity and work of the Parent-Teacher Association may be coördinated and related to its conceived functions.   Before we consider these, however, let us examine in Chapter VI the work of ten Parent-Teacher Associations in the light of the three studies referred to in this chapter.

CHAPTER VI

CASE STUDIES

A COMPREHENSIVE view of the Parent-Teacher Association would not be complete without a fairly intensive study of the Association at work. The author, realizing the difficulty of evaluating the Parent-Teacher Association through generalized observation and questionnaire treatment, decided to subject fifteen selected Parent-Teacher Associations in fifteen cities and three states to a more direct analysis. Of this number it was necessary to eliminate five for various reasons such as lack of complete records, lack of interest, and lack of coöperation. The population of the cities in which the ten case studies were made ranged from 10,000 to that of the largest city in the United States. The range of membership in the Associations studied was 70 to 600. Since the writer wished to determine to what extent the Association was functioning in the light of the purposes determined in Chapter V, the Associations finally selected were characterized as "typical"[1] in relation to present-day standards of work.

Most of the Associations were visited twice by the writer, during which time personal interviews were obtained with the presidents of the Associations and the principals of the schools. A check list[2] was used to record the practices of the organizations. An exhaustive study of purposes, programs and activities, meetings, minutes, and the reaction of the community was included in the study. Opinions of lay persons, teachers, editors of the local press, and the school superintendents were obtained. The writer believes that in every case correct interpretations of the data were made.

Table 4 summarizes the important factors of the ten case studies included by the writer in his study. Each case was measured in terms of a scale adapted from Butterworth's[3] self-administering scale. The weight of each item represents the average opinion of

[1]The ten Associations were all rated, however, as above the average by the National Congress or United Parents Associations centralized group.
[2]See Appendix, pages 123–124.
[3]Butterworth, J. E. *The Parent-Teacher Association and Its Work.* Macmillan Company, 1929.

TABLE 4

SUMMARY OF IMPORTANT FACTORS OF TEN PARENT-TEACHER ASSOCIATIONS

FACTOR	A	B	C	D	E	F	G	H	I	J
Reaction of lay people—Press	Enthusiastic	Not impressive	Has faith in P. T. A.	Not impressive	Impressive	Interested	Immediate district interested	Impressive	Enthusiastic	Fair interest
*1 Rating by responsible centralized group	Superior	Standard	Above average	Average	Superior	Good average	Above average	Above average	Superior	Superior
*2 Rating on measuring scale of this study	68	64	68½	61½	76	100	69	69	71	67
Size	150	200	175	70	700	125	380	340	300	300–325
Who initiated	Parents	Parents	Parents and school	School	School and parents	Parents and school	Parents	Parents	School	Parents and school
Per cent membership utilized in carrying on work	60	55	50–60	50	Approximately 50	55	60	48	50	45
Per cent of teacher membership	100	100	100	100	100	100	100	100	100	Few
Per cent of men	22	16	0	8	Very high family membership	About 3	50 family memberships	About 50-family membership	16	20
Per cent of attendance	70	60	59	65	50	40	55	60	55	50
Per cent of homes represented	61½	60	75	39	50	38	20	45	50	33
Size of city	Less than 5,000	Over 100,000	25,000–30,000	10,000	Over 100,000	25,000–30,000	Over 100,000	Over 100,000	10,000–25,000	Over 100,000
Personnel of membership	Average	Average	Good average	Average	Above average	Average	Good average	Above average	Good average	Average
Friction between school and Association	None	Very little	None	Difficulties easily settled	None	Very little	None	Little or none	None	Little or none
Number of meetings (regular)	10	10	8	10	8	10	8	8	7	10
Attitude of School — Leadership	Affording help	Not outstanding	Not outstanding	Not constructive enough	Guiding activities	Could help more	Some guidance	Constructive	Constructive	Helpful guidance
Attitude of School — Zeal toward P. T. A.	Helpful	Little interest	Could do more	Could do more	Helpful	Needs more	Helpful	Should initiate more work	Helpful	Real interest
Attitude of School — Friendly and coöperative	Yes	Yes	Yes	Yes	Yes	Yes, but could render more influence	Yes	Yes	Yes	Teachers should work more

Attitude of Parents and Home	Self-trained good interest	Needs training	Some training—interested	Needs training	Well trained	Needs training	Interested—some training	Improving through training	Self-trained good interest	Capable—some training
Leadership	Yes	Yes	Yes	Yes	Yes	Yes	Yes	Yes	Yes	Yes
Cooperative	Continuing	Encouraging	Continuing	Continuing	Sustained—stimulating	Encouraging	Sustained	Continuing	Stimulating	Stimulating
Interest	No	No	No	No	No	No	No	No	No	No
Dictate policies political										
Aggressive Progressive Attitude — New to support education and child welfare	Yes	Yes	Yes	Fairly so	Yes	Fairly so	Yes	Yes	Yes	Yes
In body politic	Yes	No	No	No	No	No	No	No	No	No
Strictly P.T.A. function	Yes	Yes	Yes	Yes	Yes	Yes	Yes	Yes	Yes	Yes
Committee organization	Complete	Approved	Approved	Acceptable	Complete	Approved	Approved	Approved	Complete	Complete
Publicity	Incomplete	Not organized	No definite plan	Not extensive	Incomplete	Incomplete	Incomplete	Incomplete	Not well organized	Not extensive—some attempt
Objectives	Needs restatement	Should be more defined	Well understood but not put into practice	Needs more defining of objectives	Well-defined—understood	Needs restatement of objectives	Fair understanding	Understood—needs more application	Attention given to sound objectives	Fair understanding—defined
Unified program	No	No	No	No	Some effort toward this	No	No	No	No	No
Budget policy	Not well defined	Fair—not related to activities	No definite plan	No real plan	Related to program and activities	No constructive plan	Not linked with educ. program	Fair—needs to be related to activities	Not sufficient	Attempting to correlate with program
Study groups	Well organized Should reach more	Well executed Needs more	Yes—many do not attend	Organized Needs leadership	Well planned good results Should reach more	Not sufficient Not extensive	Good—needs extension	Good and working—Needs more	Need extending—some good results	Good—many groups Needs fathers
Parent education	Indirect	Indirect—needs planning	Planned—few results	Not carefully planned	Direct plan—good results study groups	Not organized	No definite plan	Planned—fair results	Indirect	Direct and Indirect

TABLE 4—Continued

FACTOR	ASSOCIATIONS STUDIED									
	A	B	C	D	E	F	G	H	I	J
Type of activities	Educational and some non-ed.	Educational and non-ed. no plan	Educational and non-educational	All types—many non-educational	Largely educational	Many non-educational	Educational and non-educational	Largely educational	Largely educational variety	Largely educational
Results effecting desirable changes in school and community	Evidences of many	Need more effective attack	Direct evidence of many	Could be extended	Tangible and definite	Could be improved	Objective evidence of many	Clearly effective	Many evidences	Many helpful changes
Legislation program	Successful	Little or no program	Some success	None	None	None	Little or no program	Some evidences	None	None
Greatest problems of P. T. A.	Male membership—unity of program	School and community interest	Those needing Parent-ed. not attending	Father attendance—leadership	Not reaching all parents	Lack of interest in attendance	Reaching more homes—better study groups	Interest more who need Parent Ed.	Reach more parents—unified program	Teacher attendance at meetings
Method of work	Direct	Uncertain	Definite	Uncertain	Direct—certain of plan	No direct method	Not complete but organized	Direct—good plan	Definite	Definite—planned
Training of leaders	Study—central headquarters	By lectures—study—some courses	No professional courses	Self-trained	Courses—well-trained	No special training	Self-study groups	Courses for leaders	Courses planned	Self-study some professional courses
Turnover	Not large	Large	Large	Large	Not large	Large	Relatively small	Large	Not large	Not large

*1 National Congress of Parents and Teachers rates the best Associations judged in terms of standards as "Superior" Associations or "Standard" Associations.

*2 See Appendix for scale which was used to measure these Associations in terms of numerical value.

75 administrators—students at Teachers College. It does not represent the writer's personal opinion. The rank or score in Table 4 indicates the score of the ten Parent-Teacher Associations included in this study. The scores range from 60 to 76. The composite weighted judgments of 75 jurors are given on page 110.

The ten Associations show definite weaknesses in these items: "The Year's Objectives and Their Attainment," "Definite Study of Educational Needs," "Budget and the Educational Program," "Publicity," "Parent Education," "Percentage of Men Members," "Utilization of Membership," "Leadership," "Unified Program," and "Acquiring Social Power Through Participation in Public Affairs." On the other hand, there is a universal element of strength in such items as "Committee Organization," "Teacher Membership," "Meetings," "Absence of Friction," "Social Intercourse," and "Types of Activities," "Attitude of School toward the Home." All the cases show a fair organization of their Study Group work.

SUMMARY OF THE TEN CASE STUDIES

(Names of the Associations are represented by letters A to J.)

Association A

This Association in a small rural community faces problems that differ from those in a large industrial city. It is without many of the advantages found in large municipalities, such as art, science, health clinics, libraries, and the like. It, therefore, has had to put a great deal of emphasis on civic betterment projects in its program and has organized such activities as baby clinics, correction of physical defects, and research information with reference to agricultural and community work.

There are 150 members, 20 per cent of whom are men. Teacher membership is 100 per cent. Attendance is approximately 65 per cent. About one-third of the homes of the district are represented. Committee organization is well provided for. The executive committee facilitates the business of the organization. As stated above, many of the activities engaging the interest of the group are non-educational, but a good deal of energy is directed toward the consideration of major problems. There has been a definite attempt to study needs and understand what responsibilities and opportunities are those of the Parent-Teacher Association in the education of the child.

It is recommended that the Association give careful consideration to Objectives Nos. 3, 4, and 10 as set up in Chapter V in order that it may carry forward the fine work begun. It is important that this Association increase its effort to provide a general knowledge of the school philosophy, curriculum making in relation to a changing social situation, school procedures, and so forth.

Administration of relief, because of the economic stress of present conditions, has further served to diversify the activities of the group. The purchasing of equipment for the school is considered an important activity. There is independence in thought and action, and an aggressive attempt to safeguard the welfare of the child; good leadership, hard work, and coöperation have given the Association an excellent rating by the State Congress. The Association has brought about the following desirable changes:

1. Reduction of turnover.
2. Helpful educational activity; discussions of school problems such as health, curricula, recreation, etc.
3. Higher salaries for teachers.
4. Correction of health defects in pre-school children.
5. Better curriculum.
6. Better community support of schools.
7. Better housing conditions.

Some of the problems still facing the group are:

1. A need of delimiting its problems.
2. A need of a clear statement of its functions and an understanding of the community problems which lie within its province.
3. A need of integrating its activities in relation to its problems.
4. Extension of study groups to include more parents, especially men (see Appendix, page 117).

Association B

This Association, located in a large industrial city, has a cosmopolitan group of 300 members. All the teachers belong, but only 15 per cent of the members are men. The average attendance is 60 per cent. There are ten regular meetings. The only supplementary meetings are study groups of younger mothers, usually held in the homes. Leadership is above the average, many of the leaders having been specially trained.

The Association was formed to protest an undesirable use of the school building by the Board of Education. Despite such an unfortunate way of organizing, the success of the Association has been marked. Some of the activities are of the higher educational type, but they do not all achieve their purpose or function in an effective educational plan. There is a necessity, recognized by the leaders, to study the problems and needs of the community. The activities then selected, instead of being scattered as they now are, should be directed toward a solution of the immediate problems. The economic disorder of the city has also occasioned a diversification of interest, since the Association has of necessity had to aid the community in providing relief to the needy.

The local press is optimistic about the Parent-Teacher Association and the value of its news. It therefore remains the duty of the Association to embark upon a directed publicity program and to increase its prestige through the use of the press, bulletins, school paper, and other media.

There should be a greater realization of the true purposes and functions of the Parent-Teacher Association. This Association should study Objectives Nos. 3, 9, 10, and 16 listed in Chapter V. More emphasis should be placed on the objectives which give the parents a true conception of their responsibilities and opportunities in the education of the child. An extension of the Study Group plan is suggested to help achieve this end.

Friction is not a problem, and there is evidence of fine cooperation. The community has faith in the Parent-Teacher Association as evidenced by support and interest. Turnover in membership is large. There is need of greater independence in action. A unified program should be considered at once by this Association. It has the leadership, interest, and support necessary to present a splendid educational program. All that is necessary now is a formulation of problems and a relating of activity to function.

There is no evidence that the Association goes beyond its lay function. It is progressive and aggressive to support modern education and child welfare, and has supported better salaries for teachers. It has also a fine rating in the State Congress. It has brought about many desirable changes, among which we may list:

1. Greater friendliness on the part of teachers.
2. Closer coöperation on the part of the membership.
3. Good community response.
4. Training of leaders.
5. More parents interested in visiting school.

6. Special study group meetings based on the interests of certain groups.
7. Welfare work.
8. Better physical conditions for children.
9. "Room Mothers Plan" to contact school work.
10. Community program.

Special problems still facing the Association are:

1. Men membership.
2. Extension of educational activities—reduction or range of activities.
3. Unified program.
4. Publicity program.
5. Development of leaders.
6. Effective Study Group plan.

Association C

If we examine Table 4 (page 58) for the summary of Association C, we note that the 100 per cent teacher membership is offset by the fact that no men are included in the membership. The number of homes represented is high but is weakened again by the fact that men participate but little. However, men do attend meetings. The Association, working without any perceptible friction, keeps well within its province although the wide range of activities needs coördination. The many activities which the group aggressively promotes for child welfare need direction and consolidation in a program under the Unit-of-Work system. The activities are not carried to a point where they represent a concentration of interests and energies toward the solution of major problems. The Association should study its needs, recognize its problems, and organize its program.

The purchasing of equipment has not interfered with the more important major problems of the Association. The type of activities carried on by the Association has done much toward the creation of items of news value. It now remains for the Association to study avenues and devices in order to see how their usefulness may be increased. Avenues of publicity outside of the local press should be used by this Association. The legislative program is above the average. Though the Association is not political, it has been able to support favorable school legislation. There is potential leadership in this group. They have done well under the plan of self-training, but assistance from training agencies outside of their Association should be made available. There is evidence of sound business procedure. The budget of the Association is planned in the light of educational activities. There is little emphasis on money-raising activities. The study groups need extension to include more of the membership. It is suggested that one or two special groups be organized for the men of the district.

Strong Factors in the Association
1. Teacher membership.
2. Aggressiveness in work.
3. Health program.
4. Desirable changes brought about, such as:
    a) Increased teachers' salaries.
    b) Better school housing.
    c) Better police protection.
    d) Recreation periods for children.
    e) Favorable school legislation.
    f) Visiting teacher.
5. Committee work.
6. Educational activities.

Factors Still To Be Considered
1. Purposes and functions of Parent-Teacher Association.
2. Integration of activities.
3. Extension and relation of study group activities.
4. Development of a publicity program.
5. Securing of men members.
6. Means of reaching more parents.

Association D

This typical Association in a town of approximately 10,000 population has a membership of 60 or 70 members. They are of average intelligence and the morale of the group is splendid. Most of the members are women. A high percentage of attendance is evidenced, although only one-third of the homes in the school district are represented. Unfortunately, few of those attending participate in the educational program.

There would seem to be a need of more independent leadership. The school is at present too dominant a force. It has worked arduously, however, to promote the work of the Parent-Teacher Association.

There has been little attention to study groups or separate meetings organized to discuss special problems of education. What the Association needs is help from the State Congress in order to better its organization and to select its activities. It must recognize the necessity for planning its program, must then select its problem, and must finally arrange its activities in a unified program of work as suggested in Chapter VII.

The interest of the Association is good and continuous. Friction is not a problem. There has been a definite attempt to publicize its program, but there is so little understanding of that program, of proposed aims and functions, and of related activities, that the publicity work although initially good cannot follow up with constructive material. The Association is hampered by lack of training facilities for leadership. An extensive Parent Study Group plan, assisted by the State Congress, is recommended to this group to increase its number of leaders. The members usually remain in the Association as long as their children are in school. The Association is aggressive in the support of school policies and the promotion of activities which benefit the school. It keeps well within its province. It has brought about these desirable changes:

1. More friendly teachers.
2. Fewer complaints.
3. Good publicity for the school.
4. More educational equipment.
5. Relief and safety education programs.
6. Better social intercourse.

It still faces the following problems:

1. Need of understanding its own status.
2. Recognizing that Parent Education should be the first concern of the Association.
3. Selecting activities which fit the need of the community, such as Progressive Education policies, Reading Habits of Children, Interpretation of School to Community.
4. Need of exercising leadership independent of the school.
5. Lack of unit program and the consolidation of activities under major problems.
6. Training leadership.

Association E

The problems of this Association are sharply contrasted to those in the average public school. It is part of a progressive experimental school and located in a very large city. Its membership is 700. The personnel is above the average in intelligence, interest, and leadership. Children are drawn mainly from professional classes which include a preponderant number of educators and teachers. The percentage of attendance is 50 per cent. The percentage of homes represented is 50 per cent. Teachers are represented 100 per cent. This Association has the family membership plan, meaning that both parents are included in the membership upon payment of stipulated dues. Thus, the father's representation equals that of the mother. Six regular meetings are held each year, attended by a large proportion of the membership. Many special meetings are held to provide for the interests and needs of those concerned. The leadership of the school is excellent and well informed on modern educational theory and practice. Many leaders in this Association have been trained professionally. There is less than the usual friction between school and home. The action of the Association is characterized by independence of thought and no attempt is made to dictate the policies of the school. The Association is progressive and aggressive in support of child welfare.

In order to make sure the Association would have clearly in mind the objectives of the Parent-Teacher Association and understand its true functions, the leadership initiated the Association after many discussions and meetings. Organization was not perfected until five years after the first proposal that a Parent-Teacher Association be organized in this school. An early view of its philosophy and policy may be seen in the following statement:

If we organize a Parent-Teacher Association it could function as an educational medium for teachers and parents through an exchange of views both as to modern problems as they bear upon education, and specifically as to matters relating to the school itself.

All this was done to educate the membership in regard to the potential power of the Association. These meetings were characterized as ones calling for less immediate action but more careful study, leading to an understanding of the aims of the Association. Needs were studied, interests and activities classified. Eventually the Association was organized.

Since many of its pupils come from various sections of a large city and some from other cities, it is not called upon to serve a particular community in the sense in which the average Parent-Teacher Association is forced to serve. It is, however, exerting an influence on the several communities by its program of parent education and by its emphasis on units of study which have broad social significance.

The Association tries to carry out its purposes by the use of a very complete plan of parent-study groups. Here the parents are homogeneously grouped according to interest and understanding. Such groups aim for close coöperation and understanding in every grade. "Grade Representatives" relieve teachers of the mechanics of setting up these meetings but teachers are a part of the plan and program. Such groups are directed by a competent person who endeavors to "tie up" the subject matter of the various groups with the larger meetings. The excellent results of such studies should be made available to other groups outside of this organization.

While the activities are mainly educational and groups are divided according to interests, there is much that can be done to unify and coördinate the program. Many of the activities, accumulative in character, can be developed into larger and more helpful units. Discussion of fundamentals in education is attempted with good success. Much more could be done with the local press and by the use of bulletins, school news, and papers to build up a constructive publicity program along the lines suggested in Chapter IV.

The Association is securing excellent returns for the investment it has made, because of a careful study of problems together with a persistent effort to plan a program to solve these problems.

Outstanding Features of "E" Association

1. Cumulative discussions of problems.
2. Broad social aspect of work.
3. Consideration of fundamental problems in education.
4. Parent Education program by use of extensive study groups plan.
5. Active interest of fathers (the large study group composed of fathers is unique).
6. Parents grouped according to interests and needs to consider delimited problems.
7. Financial support on the part of school and membership.
8. Leadership—personnel.
9. Continued interest and coöperation.

Recommendations

1. Extension of study group plan and cumulative discussion of various topics to take the form of larger units of study. There should be a definite controlling theme set up as an objective toward which such groups with the proper direction can well make a contribution.

2. More parents should receive the benefit of the Association work. Attendance in study groups should be increased.

3. Study plans of the Association should continue to interest the fathers. The experiment with this group should be made available to other Parent-Teacher Associations.

4. There is need for a more definite "tie-up" between the component parts of the Association, such as committee work, study groups, and general meetings of the entire membership.

5. Meetings of the entire group should be increased in number.

Association F

The Association in this residential town of about 25,000 population is unique in the extent and the diversification of its activities. The personnel consists of a mixed group such as is usually found in a small city or a community, the population of which is for the most part American. Of the membership, which is about 100, only two per cent are men. Only one-third of the homes of the district are represented.

Ten regular meetings are held each year. One child-study group meets several times a year. The number of activities carried on by the Association is too great to list. Many of these activities should be abandoned or consolidated and organized under the Unit-of-Work plan suggested in Chapter VII. The child-study group should be greatly extended to include a careful study of subjects and activities interesting to and within the comprehension of the group.

Real parent education and an interpretation regarding the possibilities of modern education are extremely necessary to this group and will be achieved easily through a planning of the work under the unit idea. It must be worked out coöperatively and the activities selected must conform to the interests, understanding, and satisfaction of the group. Such a plan would also serve the purpose of discouraging the attendance of children at the regular Association meetings.

The Association should devote some time to a consideration of the functions and purposes of the Parent-Teacher Association as listed in Chapter V. In the opinion of the writer, special emphasis should be placed on Objectives Nos. 2, 3, 4, 9, and 10.

In the working of the organization some friction has been evidenced, but this is not now apparent. Instead we find good coöperative effort. The reaction of the community to the Association is good.   The 100 per cent teacher membership also indicates interest and coöperation on the part of the school.   Although the committee organization is very complete, the large number of standing committees does not result in a high utilization of membership.   The recommendations above with regard to study groups and unit programs will undoubtedly solve this difficulty. Further difficulties may be listed as follows:

1. Lack of independence in thought and action.   The Parent-Teacher Association officers lean on the leadership and policies of the school.
2. Need of leaders trained in professional training courses.

Desirable changes that have been brought about are:

1. Better school equipment.
2. Safety education.
3. Health program and playground.
4. More friendly teachers.
5. Parents better informed regarding school procedure.

There is still much to be done, however.   Undoubtedly the efficiency and value of the group will be increased by an adoption of the Unit-of-Work program as suggested above.   In addition, the following are also recommended for the Association:

1. Extension of publicity program.
2. Increased attendance.
3. Reduction of turnover in membership.
4. More initiative in effecting needed reforms, e.g. good school legislation, new education, teachers' salaries, etc.

Association G

Association G is located in a large city in which the Parent-Teacher Association is not popular and where, because the movement is viewed with suspicion, few of the city's 75 schools have such organizations.   The problems of this group are those of a large cosmopolitan group in a large city.   The membership of 380 is according to family and thus about 50 per cent of the members are men.   Teachers are 100 per cent in membership, and about one-third of the homes in the district are represented.   Attendance is about 50 per cent. The personnel is above the average.   Many Jewish families are represented.   Meetings occur regularly eight times a year and are supplemented by a number of child-study groups.

In spite of the poor support given to the Parent-Teacher Association in this city, this Association has an adequate knowledge of its purposes and functions and is performing excellent if undirected work in Parent Education. The officers should, however, discuss with the members Objectives Nos. 3, 4, 9, 10, and 16 listed in Chapter V in order to improve and integrate the yearly program. Much more could be done to reduce the number of activities or to consolidate them under one major idea or unit. Directing the enthusiasm and energy of every member would result in a definition of the major problems of the group and a concerted drive toward the solution of that problem.

Committee work is planned according to state suggestions. A unification of this work under the Unit-of-Work system would result in a greater understanding of desired ends, and would increase the possibility of achieving those ends. The budget committee's plans need reorganization; for example, in order to make adequate provision for the educational activities which the group desires to pursue. The publicity set-up could be improved and extended along the lines suggested in Chapter IV. Leadership is good and is well supported. There is, however, need for training. The parents and the school evidence a fine aggressive attitude and do not allow politics to interfere with independent thought and action. Membership is fairly constant. The Association has achieved the following desirable changes:

1. Increase in teachers' salaries.
2. Better housing conditions for the school (the Association influenced the building of one school).
3. Respect of the entire community toward the Association.
4. Playgrounds.
5. Health program, child hygiene program.
6. Parent education plan.
7. Child study groups.
8. Fewer complaints.
9. Better morale in the district.
10. Better police protection.

It still faces the following problems:

1. Necessity for extending the work to affect more homes.
2. Adoption of Unit program to meet the need for unification of activities.
3. Necessity for training in leadership.
4. Extension of publicity program.
5. Participation of members at meetings and the promotion of organized discussion.

Association H

This Association in a large city has an excellent personnel, all types of people comprising its membership. There are over 300 family memberships, although few men participate in the activities to any great extent. All teachers of the school belong and about one-third of the homes are represented. Attendance at meetings is about 60 per cent.

There are eight regular meetings and these are supplemented by many study groups. The subject matter and activities are largely educational with an emphasis on cultural programs. There is some evidence that a study of problems and needs has been made. This is due to well-trained leadership of parents, which is far above the average. The avenue which provides for these needs is the study group plan, directed by competent leaders. The Association is reaching out for information relative to the things which pertain to parent and child education. What is necessary now is a consideration in detail by the group of Objectives Nos. 10, 11, and 16 as listed in Chapter V. There is indication of an intelligent conception of aims and purposes of Parent-Teacher Associations, but the activities which are carried on to attain these purposes although educational are neither directed nor integrated.

The business of the group is conducted competently by the executive committee. Budget procedure is sound and educational planning has influenced its construction. Friction is not a problem. The school and home seem to be coöperative, and the morale is high. When child welfare is at stake, the Association is aggressive in its support. It is also progressive in its outlook and is independent in thought and action. Publicity activities are neither extensive nor well considered. Desirable changes brought about by the Association include:

1. Program for the study of Mental Hygiene.
2. Closer articulation of school and home.
3. Development of leadership.
4. Health program.
5. Effective study-group plan.

There are, however, still facing the Association the following problems:

1. Development of the men's interest in the work of the Parent-Teacher Association.

2. Further training in leadership.

3. An adequate publicity set-up and a study of publicity problems as suggested in Chapter IV.

4. An integration of program activities so that there is a closer coördination between functions and activities. This may be accomplished under the Unit-of-Work system outlined in Chapter VII.

Association I

This Association, located in a city of 24,000 population, is unique in its energetic attempt to include a number of activities, most of which are educational and helpful to the school and community. Although much time is given to community problems, such as relief (because of economic conditions), use of leisure, and group coöperation in promoting educational activities, this does not interfere with a splendid Parent Education program, a major aim of the Association and one for which there is a budgetary allowance.

There are 300 members, holding seven regular meetings a year. Various groups are represented in the personnel, and the percentage of attendance is 55 per cent. All teachers are members. The percentage of father members is 16. The number of homes represented is nearly 50 per cent. Leadership in both the Association and the school is above the average, and though there is some attempt further to train leaders, this is hampered by lack of training facilities and opportunities.

The Association might do well to discuss at length the objectives Nos. 3, 4, and 10, listed in Chapter V. When those aims are comprehended by the entire Association there would probably be some shifting of interest and energy relative to the activities considered. There is need in this group of a closer integration of the activities carried on. The excellent educational work done by the group would be more effective and could easily be blocked out, under a central idea or theme, to give a complete understanding of an idea or theme and its relation to a great number of allied interests which are at present considered independently. Such an integration of activities would give the membership a clear, convincing picture of its own problems and the methods and materials necessary to solve those problems. Committee work is well planned, and under the unit system the twelve study groups which consider educational problems could be organized to discuss concomitant problems or contribute to a more detailed study of the larger problems of the entire organization.

Not enough work is done with publicity although a start has been made. The reaction of the press is favorable and the community thinks well of this group and gives them much support. Part of this favorable community attitude is undoubtedly explained by the fact that the Association keeps well within its lay function and does not try to dictate school or educational policies. The turnover in membership is not large. The Association is rated high by the State Congress of Parents and Teachers. It has achieved the following desirable changes:

1. Health program in school, including nutrition work.
2. Correction of physical defects of the pre-school child.
3. Emergency relief.
4. Playgrounds.
5. Better use of leisure time on the part of parents and children.
6. Better morale in school and community.
7. Extension of music program.
8. More interest in and support of schools.

Special problems are:

1. Small membership of men.
2. Excessive number of activities.
3. Lack of courses in the training of leadership.
4. Lack of a complete publicity program.
5. Getting more of the membership to work.
6. Increasing representation of homes in district.
7. Lack of a unified program.

Association J

This Association, located in a very large city, has a membership of about 300. Its personnel, through hard work and splendid coöperation and interest, have succeeded in bringing about many desirable changes in relation to general child welfare. Of the membership, 20 per cent are men but the percentage of teacher members is conspicuously low. The percentage of homes represented is about 33 per cent. Attendance is approximately 50 per cent. Only about one-half of the membership is used in carrying out program activities and Association plans. There are ten regular meetings in the year, as well as many special meetings in the form of study groups.

Leadership is above the average. Some training is provided for leaders of special study groups. There is little or no friction in any of the groups. Committee organization is well planned, most business procedure being carried on at executive meetings. The Association stays within its lay function and does not trespass on the professional functions of the school. Little constructive work has been done with publicity. Although activities are educational, there is a need of consolidation into a unified program of parent education. The Association has studied its problems. It now needs to select those of major concern and direct its activities toward a solution of those problems. The budget policy is improving and an attempt is being made to include items for the advancement of an educational program.

The officers are conversant with the true functions of the Parent-Teacher Association. It is now necessary that they spend more time in interpreting these to the members. Discussion and report at group meetings of Objectives Nos. 3, 4, 9, 10, and 11 as listed in Chapter V would be helpful. The desirable changes which the Association has produced are:

1. A high type of education to understand the work of the school.
2. Fewer complaints.
3. More friendly teachers and parents.
4. Better health conditions.
5. A program of playgrounds and recreation.
6. Boys clubs.

It still faces the following problems:

1. Poor interest on the part of the teachers,—the excellent leadership in the school could be used to obtain greater coöperation on the part of the teachers.
2. Failure to extend its work to include more of its membership.
3. Lack of a unified program and a consolidation of activities under one theme or unit. Such a program should be introduced only when a study of the Association's needs has been made.

SUMMARY AND CONCLUSIONS

In general it may be said that the findings of this more intensive study of the work of the Parent-Teacher Association, as indicated in the reports on each of the Associations, A to J, as well as by data in Table 4, bear out the findings of the more generalized study of one hundred Associations throughout the United States. Each Association keeps well within its lay function, but there is too wide a range of activities. In the cases studied there seems to be some recognition of the fact that the value of educational activities was being endangered by the large number of non-educational, activities, but there was little attempt to do anything about it. The situation is almost uniformly explainable by the lack of information about scientific program planning. Only one organization showed an attempted unification of its program activities and it was not markedly successful.

The major need of these ten Associations is consolidation of their activities and unification of their program in the manner described in Chapter VII. This admission, however, only reveals a deeper need of the Parent-Teacher Association: that of more highly trained leadership from its own ranks and of other skilled counsellors especially trained to function in this field. It is imperative on the one hand that colleges and training schools undertake to provide training for officers and committee chairmen of these Associations, and just as imperative on the other that the school system itself take the initiative in securing the services of skillful individuals who would assume the responsibility of studying the family background of children and its relation to the child's work in school, and assist parents and teachers in the study of their problems.[4] The combination would inevitably bring about the unification of program and activities absolutely essential if the Parent-Teacher Association is to be really serviceable to parents and the schools.

Most of the Associations are reducing the purchasing of equipment for the schools to a point where it does not interfere to any great extent with their educational programs. The use of publicity to secure community support for its programs has not been developed by any of the Associations. Study groups are a major activity but they fail to reach enough parents. The Associations should study carefully the relationship between the school administration and Parent-Teacher Association as outlined in Chapter III. A real financial plan designed to affect all the activities of the Association is another vital necessity.

[4]Cf. Chapter I, page 15.

CHAPTER VII

THE UNIT OF WORK IN PROGRAM PLANNING FOR THE PARENT-TEACHER ASSOCIATION

SINCE it has been demonstrated in preceding chapters that the energies and interests of the local Associations are dispersed over a wide range of unrelated and undirected activity, this chapter is designed to suggest a method of unifying and integrating program work in the Parent-Teacher Association. It will be necessary first to show the underlying principles of a program of work for the Association; second, to show the futility and ineffectiveness of the present program found in the average Association; and, third, to recommend a plan for unifying the program under one general theme covering a certain period of time and based on carefully investigated needs of the community.

Program making has not been sufficiently studied by Parent-Teacher Association leaders. The art of planning and preparing, in an interesting manner with an end in view, related topics from which members will be able to acquire ideas, conceptions, and important understandings is conspicuously absent from most Parent-Teacher Association programs. M. B. Mason[1] has this to say regarding the preparation of a program:

A plan is a real thing. It comes before action, just as the conception and drawing of a house come before the building of it. Even with knowledge and enthusiasm the making of plans is the most difficult task that confronts the leader. It requires thought to make a plan and thinking is our hardest job. Knowledge of facts can be acquired by any one. Upon the leader's ability to think out a plan depends a large measure of success of his Association.

Such planning is undoubtedly indispensable to the successful Parent-Teacher Association. Yet good planning of work presupposes that an effort has been made to determine the relationship of its aims and purposes to its greatest problems. Real planning indicates the power to see the plans through. It involves comprehension of purpose, location of problem, selection

[1]Mason, M. B. *Parents and Teachers.* Ginn and Company, New York, 1928. Page 244.

of activities, and a consolidation of those activities under a series of worthwhile experiences.

In studying the work of one hundred Associations, the writer found that the most disturbing thing to both the administrator and the Parent-Teacher Association official was the organization and presentation of a well-balanced program which not only would explain the worthy objects of the Association but would really educate the members in the matters taken up for consideration. Many Association presidents, who had a critical understanding of their work, traced their difficulties directly or indirectly to a faulty and ineffectual program set-up. The writer found that Association after Association, capable of performing an outstanding piece of work under able leadership, lost sight of its major responsibility because the random activities selected unwisely by the Association and related only remotely to any one of the major functions failed to bring satisfaction to the members or to realize the real function of the Parent-Teacher Association.

It is possible to combine real interest with persistent effort on the part of the members and yet to achieve nothing of appreciable value to the membership or the community because neither the interest nor the effort is properly directed. Unity of purpose, idea, and activity is required for worth-while work.

It was shown in Chapter V that parent education is considered by Parent-Teacher Association leaders and students of education to be a function of major importance to the Association, and that the development of intelligent parents with an understanding of the problems of childhood and education is an objective toward which most of the activity of the Association should be directed. Therefore, bearing in mind the needs and limitations of each Association or community, all leaders, committees, and groups, using every available means, should work toward that objective. The leaders must be encouraged to identify and delimit their problems. They must be given the technique which will help them initiate and develop a program of work which is within the limits of the understanding of the group. And a plan must be developed to challenge the interest of the Association and to provide for its needs.

The National Congress of Parents and Teachers defines "Program" thus:

The annual program of a Parent-Teacher Association is its general plan of work to meet the needs of the home, the school, and the community as they relate to the welfare of the child. The object of the program is to enable members of the Association to realize conditions or discover needs; to formulate plans to meet those needs; and to stimulate action which will produce the desired changes.

Under this generalized definition, however, the Associations have put all those undirected activities which were considered in preceding chapters. Failure to understand the importance of a good unified program has resulted in hit-or-miss planning. This faulty planning, lack of organization, and the absence of a good technique in devising programs result in a weakening of the contribution which even desirable activities could make to the education of the parents and their understanding of what they are trying to do.

On page 80 is a typical program showing all the faults mentioned above. There is in it very little attempt to coördinate or consolidate the activities of the Association, and almost no recognition of the fact that there is a goal toward which to work.

Some of the better local Associations have added to their programs a detailed outline of subjects under discussion with questions to provoke thought and interest. The program on page 81, from Saginaw, Michigan, illustrates an evening's program.

This program is illustrative of a step in the right direction toward planned programs of directed activity. But it represents one example of this as contrasted with an array of inefficiency and undirected energy.

Since there exists this general inefficiency, this undirected activity, a method of planning a Unit of Work with the purpose of eliminating uncoördinated programs foreign to the needs of the community is proposed for Parent-Teacher Associations. The Unit of Work Plan is familiar to educators and is already widely and successfully used in many schools throughout the United States.[2] The application of this method to the Parent-Teacher Association is new but it seems to offer the best solution to its problems of program planning.

It may be objected that such a comprehensive plan is not

[2]Notably the schools of South Dakota, organized under the direction of Dr. Herbert B. Bruner of Teachers College, Columbia University, and the social studies work for grades seven, eight, and nine prepared by Dr. Harold Rugg.

PROGRAM OF—— PARENT-TEACHER ASSOCIATION 1930–1931

Tues., Sept. 29—Open Meeting 3:15

Tues., Oct. 20—3:15 P.M.
MEMBERSHIP RALLY
Discussions:
"Why Be a Member of the P.T.A."
"What Membership in the P.T.A.
Should Mean."
Refreshments.

Tues., Jan. 18—3:00 P.M.
Dental Hygiene
Toothbrush Drill by School Children
Supervisor of Dental Hygiene will
discuss "Dental Hygiene."
Regular Meeting.

Tues., Feb. 16—3:15 P.M.
Founders' Day. Speaker, Junior
Supervisor of Adult Education.
Candle Lighting Ceremony.
Music. Refreshments.

Tues., March 15—2:35 P.M.
Seventh Grade Entertains P.T.A.
Members to be guests of seventh
grade class.
School work of Grades 6 and 7 to be
exhibited in the hall.
Refreshments will be served.

Fri., Nov. 20—Fathers' Night Pro-
gram by School Children.
Fathers are especially urged to attend.
Speaker.

Tues., December 15.
Christmas Spirit: Carol Singing.
Discussions by Mothers—
"The Best Gift for Boy or Girl."
Speaker, subject, "Good Books."
Book List.

Tues., April 19—3:15 P.M.
The Problem Child.
Speaker, School Psychologist.
Opportunity for questions.
School work of grades 3, 4, 5 and
special group will be exhibited.

Tues., May 18—7:30 P.M.
Fathers' Night.
Business Meeting.
Program by school children, 8:00
P.M. Speaker, Principal; Subject,
"School."
The art work of grades 4 to 7 will be
exhibited in the halls.

Tues., June 7—3:15 P.M.
Annual Meeting.
Reports of Standing Committees and
election of officers.
School work of kindergarten and grades
1 and 2 will be exhibited.
Refreshments will be served.

SPECIAL EVENTS TO REMEMBER
October 30, 1:30–4:30 o'clock—Food Sale
Week of November 9—Education Week.
The school will issue invitations for parents to visit.
Wednesday evening, March 24—P.T.A. Good Time—
(Party for Mothers and Fathers)

suited to the needs of a voluntary organization with a shifting
personnel, in which the participation of the majority of members is usually limited to listening. The answer to this objec-
tion is that the use of this very plan does much to eliminate

October 15, 1931

Topic: "How Children Differ Mentally and the Effect upon the Changing Drama of Behavior."

Questions for thought and discussion

1. If a child whom you had always considered bright began to be indifferent to his school work and to create trouble in the schoolroom, what are the things you would try to find out about him?

2. What is being done in the schools of your community for:
   A. Subnormal children?
   B. Especially bright children?
   C. Children who have behavior difficulties?

3. Mention some of the dangers of too great freedom and independence in early childhood.

Suggestions for further reading

Arlitt, Ada H. *The Child from One to Six.* New York, McGraw Hill, 1930.

Hollingworth, Harry L. *Mental Growth and Decline.* New York, Appleton, 1927.

Woodrow, Herbert L. *Brightness and Dullness in Children.* Philadelphia, Lippincott, 1923.

---

these characteristics of the ordinary Association. This is not only theoretically but actually the case. The scheme has been used with outstanding results in Passaic, New Jersey, where it has reduced turnover in membership, and shifting attendance at meetings, and has drawn into participation in activities far more persons than under the previous type of program planning.

It needs only a moment's reflection to see why this is the case. That parents want education has been established by the educational authorities to whom we have referred in these pages; that this desire for learning taps one of the deepest instinctive drives of human nature also goes without question. Meager nourishment in response to this need has so far been supplied by the Parent-Teacher Association, but despite the poverty of its educational program millions of parents have been only too eager to accept even these crumbs of knowledge. All that is here proposed is that a comprehensive plan be adopted which takes consciously into account the real desire of parents to enrich and expand both their information and their opportunities for using it.

UNIT OF WORK PLAN

We may define the Unit of Work for the Parent-Teacher Association as the organization of a block of related material on any topic or group of topics in such form that everything the Parent-Teacher Association does in developing its program contributes toward the understanding of a central idea and its relation to other concepts in the same or allied fields. The adaptation of such a plan to Parent-Teacher Association work will enable the members to see more clearly the purposes of the Association and to understand why certain subjects or ideas are developed in the course of their programs.

The adoption of the Unit of Work as the program plan involves a high degree of thoroughness in the work of the Association. Clarity of purpose, concentration, coöperation must be exhibited by all members, leaders, groups, and committees. Committees on finance, membership, program, publicity, child welfare, and so forth, must harmonize their efforts into an integrated whole, and work toward one common purpose. Interest, leadership, hard work, and coöperative effort in unified activity should result in an educational experience for the membership which will include new information, changes in attitudes, a wider appreciation of the problems of public education, and more intelligent support for it.

Chart I shows how various activities may be consolidated and unified to make one larger whole or unit. To make the unit complete, enough selected and properly organized activities should be included. In a unit of work of any kind, objectives, approaches, analysis of problems, local needs, points of view are indispensable.

It must be remembered that the unit in itself when organized will accomplish little. Its effectiveness rests on the earnestness, industry, and intelligence of those who work in it. Properly organized and administered, the unit plan of work should be a valuable tool, whose intelligent use will enable local Associations to approach a realization of their true functions and purposes.

Chart II gives a proposed graphic representation of the unit which is described in the succeeding pages.

Every unit proposed for the Parent-Teacher Association must include a statement of the aims based on carefully thought-out needs. Care must be taken to see that all topics and activities selected are those which will be interesting to the parents. The unit must be outlined in detail and an analysis of all possible approaches included. There should also be a wide range of topics for discussion.

The topics subjected to study and research either by experts or by capable parents or teachers should be presented to the Association with the highest degree of simplicity and clarity in order that all members may grasp the theme back of them. Im-

CHART I

DIAGRAM OF PLAN OF WORK FOR PARENT-TEACHER
ASSOCIATIONS

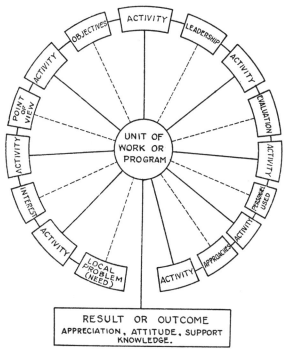

The diagram presented here shows how the activities must be employed to carry out a unified program. Activities must be cumulative and consolidated through the proper employment of Leadership, Objectives, Point of View, Local Need, Approach, Personnel, etc., to secure desired results.

portant considerations in organizing the program for the Association are:

1. How are the topics for consideration to be selected?

2. Are they interesting to the membership? Will a discussion of such topics benefit the membership?

CHART II

GRAPHICAL REPRESENTATION OF IMPORTANT STEPS IN ORGANIZING A UNIT

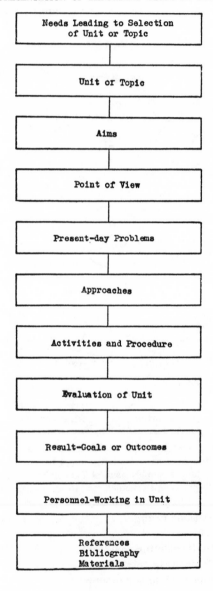

Needs Leading to Selection
of Unit or Topic

Unit or Topic

Aims

Point of View

Present-day Problems

Approaches

Activities and Procedure

Evaluation of Unit

Result-Goals or Outcomes

Personnel-Working in Unit

References
Bibliography
Materials

3. Are they within the understanding of the group and adaptable to their needs?

4. Does the presentation of program appeal to the group?

5. Does the group considering the program represent various points of view?

6. Are the topics of practical application?

7. Are the topics intrinsically worth while and significant?

8. What topics or subjects should be considered at separate group meetings?

Facts, incidents, knowledge, information, experience, opinions, illustrations, and interpretations must all be a part of the preliminary report before an Association can safely select the unit which is to occupy its attention for a period of time.

All the above items must be considered in selecting the unit about which the Association is to center its activities. The task of preparing a definite unit of work is one of great importance. Any unit extending over a period of time and utilizing the personnel of an Association, its interests, energies, and leadership, can justify its existence only in terms of concrete results. The problems of the community, if not immediately obvious to the membership, must be identified by research and study and catalogued in order of importance. From this list the problem which represents the most urgent need of the community should be selected as the subject of immediate attack.

Directing all its energies, activities, and interests toward the solution of a specific problem, the Association should use every means to settle the difficulty at hand.

Some units which may be valuable are suggested in the following list:

1. The wise use of children's leisure time.
2. Systematic health training.
3. Character training.
4. Worthy home membership.
5. Study habits of children.
6. Fitting the child for an occupation.
7. Reading habits.
8. How children learn.
9. How good citizenship is acquired.
10. Fads and frills in education.
11. The machine age and the school.

12. Home work.

13. Study of parents' attitude toward sex problems of childhood.

14. Education in relation to vocational problems.

15. New methods in discipline.

16. The extra-curricular activities.

17. Educational and vocational guidance.

18. The cost of public school education.

Around any one of these suggested units may be constructed a course of activity and study to hold the attention of the Parent-Teacher Association for any specified length of time. A working outline of a unit of work as carried on by the Woodrow Wilson Parent-Teacher Association in Passaic, New Jersey, is included here. This will serve as an illustration of the method of using this system better than any theoretical description.

UNIT OF WORK AS CARRIED OUT IN THE WOODROW WILSON SCHOOL PARENT-TEACHER ASSOCIATION—PASSAIC, NEW JERSEY

"WHAT IS BEING DONE FOR CHILDREN TO-DAY IN THE MODERN SCHOOLS"
(A Unit of Parent Education)

Time—Ten months.

NEED OF PROBLEM

Why was unit selected? Parents were indifferent to general attack on education. In many directions new educational theory was questioned, many were willing to turn back the progress made in education. Retrenchment at all costs seemed to be the byword. Many held schools responsible for the educational ills of civilization and present economic and social life. Lack of interest and understanding in school activity and school problems was evident.

GENERAL OBJECTIVE FOR UNIT OF WORK

1. To show what the modern school is doing and why.

SPECIFIC OBJECTIVES

1. To understand the general aims of education.

2. To appreciate the changes in civilization and how the school is meeting these changes.

3. To appreciate the importance of such types of educational service as vocational education, the fine arts, and their relation to life and the formal subjects of the curriculum.

4. To learn of the claims and results of the progressive schools, to know what experimental schools are doing; how such methods may be adapted to the public school.

5. To appreciate the need of schools; education as an investment, to safeguard our civilization.

POINT OF VIEW

Life changes. Therefore business, industry and the schools must change. A new school with new courses of study, up-to-date methods, must be employed to meet these changes in life. A complex society including a disintegrated family life as well as the technical machine age has thrust upon the school many new problems. What is the modern school doing to justify its existence in the light of added responsibilities?

PRESENT PROBLEMS

1. Lack of school support in its various activities.
2. Reduction in school appropriations.
3. Failure of men to participate in Parent-Teacher Association work.
4. Large number of foreign-born parents.
5. Lack of knowledge regarding the traditions and ideals of America.
6. Lack of initiative to interest themselves in school problems, such as financial support or curricula.
7. Ignorance of school procedure.

POSSIBLE APPROACHES

1. Discuss changing civilization necessitating a changing school.
2. Study what pupils do when they leave school.
3. Discuss the value of the right kind of education; what the school can do about it.
4. Consider the effects of the machine age.
5. Discuss education as an investment.
6. Discuss the curriculum of the school.

ACTIVITIES TO BE USED

ORIENTATION—DRAMATIZATION—OBSERVATION—GROUP DISCUSSION

Orientation Activities

MARCH

1. Talk by principal on the aims of education—"Which Way Is Education Headed?"
2. Talk by President of the Board of Education—"Administering the Modern School."

Dramatization Activities

APRIL

1. Discussion of the aims of education by lay leader and supervisor in public schools. Topics to be discussed are:
   a) Definition of education.
   b) Aims—past and present.
   c) Present-day curricula—The New School.

d) Educational results.
e) Supervision.
f) Financial support.
g) School control—The Pupil's Responsibility.
h) Lectures by superintendent of schools and community leader—
"Education as an Investment"; "A Community Without Schools."

Observation Activities

MAY

1. Demonstration of classroom recitation—points to be covered:
a) Method of presentation.
b) Subject matter selected.
c) Rôle of the teacher.
d) Management and organization.
e) Practical application.

JUNE

Subject—School Control; Pupils Learn by Doing.   Reports by pupils on:
a) Self Government.
b) Clubs.
c) School Papers.
d) Classroom Procedure.
e) Athletics and Games.
f) Safety Education.

OCTOBER

A committee should be delegated to visit a progressive experimental school
and report its observations to the general meeting of the Association.

NOVEMBER

Visit to school by parents under supervision of principal. (Note: This
visit is to give parents a perspective of the work of the school but it is not to
include a study of classroom method, which is a professional function).

DECEMBER

The Fine Arts: Exhibit, Explanation and Lecture.   Correlation with other
subjects.

JANUARY

1. Guidance.
2. Vocational courses.
3. Preparation for life work.
4. Fitting courses to the needs of pupils.

FEBRUARY

Education as an investment.   Debate: superintendent of schools and lay
leader.

MARCH

Summary and Conclusions of Unit. Report by committee made up of representatives of the various groups.

EVALUATION—RESULTS OR OUTCOMES

1. Does the unit suggest problems for further study which can be discussed at the meetings of various study groups?
2. Is there more interest in the Association?
3. Is there more interest in education and the schools?
4. Is there a better attendance?
5. Is there more social intercourse, more friendly relations?
6. Has there been more opportunity for leadership?
7. Are more members participating in Association work?
8. Are there more men in attendance?
9. Is there more community support of schools?
10. Has the membership acquired important information?
11. Is there a better attitude toward and appreciation of modern education?

PERSONNEL PARTICIPATING IN THE UNIT

1. Parent-Teacher Association membership
   a) President and committees.
   b) State Congress representative.
2. School principal
   a) Staff of teachers.
   b) Clerical force—to assemble important conclusions.
   c) Pupils.
3. Special lecturers
   a) Educational experts within and out of school system.
   b) Lay leadership.
4. Board of Education group
   a) Superintendent of schools.
   b) President of the board.

MATERIALS TO BE USED

1. *Reports* of the Progressive Education Association.
2. *Reports* of Lincoln School, New York City.
3. *Middletown*, Lynds.
4. *Changing Civilization*, Kilpatrick.
5. National Education Association *Reports*.
6. Local course of study of public school.
7. *Schools of Tomorrow*, Dewey.
8. *The Great Technology*, Rugg.

The following is suggested by the author as another possible type of unit and the way in which it might be worked out. It is valuable, of course, only as an example. It is necessary for each Association to decide on its own unit and the methods of working out its program.

ACQUAINTING THE PARENT WITH THE WORK OF THE NEW SCHOOL
(A UNIT OF PARENT EDUCATION)

THE CONTROLLING THEME

The development of a new school to meet a changing social order. The chief aim of this unit of work is to assist parents in an understanding of the changes which have been made in the school curriculum to meet the demands of our changing social order. It would result in giving them a dynamic concept of education, in the light of which the futility of the methods of the old school when applied to changed conditions in modern society would be apparent, and the existence of new content, organization, and procedure in the new school understood.

AIMS

A. To help parents understand the concept of social change.
B. To help parents realize the social situation of to-day, economically, politically, and socially. This would embrace an understanding of the changing function of the family.
C. To show how the present social situation affects education:[1]
  1. The problems it raises for the modern school.
  2. The expansion of curriculum that results from an attempt to meet these problems.
  3. The necessity for a new type of training for teachers.
  4. The dependence of the new school on community faith and support.

POINT OF VIEW

Formerly education was concerned with smaller and more restricted groups. Pupils of ability were taken care of in restricted fields while the untrained majority were sent into society to do what they could. For those in the schools there was very little need of differentiation in subject matter because specialization was not practiced to any great extent. Pupils who could not adapt themselves to a regular course of study were dropped as failures and they made for themselves uncertain places in society. The machine age, the growth of the factory system, the division of labor, and the consequent emphasis on specialization have made the schools aware of a new social order and forced them to meet these changes in society by compensating changes in the school system, by differentiating their courses, by changing their curricula, and by adding prevocational and vocational courses. In addition, they have made provision for guidance, appreciation, and experience courses, teaching the wise use of leisure time. The responsibility now thrust upon

[1]This would involve developing some comprehension of the philosophy, methods, curriculum and organization of the old school.

the schools by church, home, and society in general has resulted in these very necessary changes in curricula.

It is necessary, therefore, that the parent understand the organization, problems, and plans of the new school. A discussion of the problems suggested below will help the parents toward this understanding and will at the same time show them their place in the educational life of the child under these new conditions. Problems suggested will, of course, reflect specific community needs and should therefore originate with the members of the Parent-Teacher Association themselves.

PRESENT-DAY PROBLEMS

1. Persistent reverence for the Three R's—ultra-conservatism.
2. Indifference of public to function of the school.
3. Inability to recognize real teaching.
4. Failure on the part of some people to appreciate the new and special functions of the school.
5. Low salaries for teachers; mismanagement of government tax levies.
6. Ignorance of the public as to school methods.
7. Failure of the administrator properly to use and work with community leadership.
8. The changing function of the family and family relationships.
9. Improper use of leisure time.
10. Pernicious effect of tabloid, movie, etc.
11. Technological processes and effect on school and community.
12. Proper school support.
13. Misfits in society.

APPROACH

Having now selected the unit, having decided upon the aims and points of view, having also decided upon the specific problems which relate to the particular Association, the unit may be organized. Associations should be extremely careful about the manner of this organization. The approach determines the success or failure of the unit. An initial discussion to challenge the interest of the parent and to show how the subjects to be considered are related to the life of the member is pertinent. It is imperative that the approach be adapted to a particular community and considered in the light of the parents' comprehension and experience. A right approach will make the parents work for their Association, will stimulate interest in the activity under the unit plan, and will produce the best final results of the work.

Approaches may be selected from the following questions which should stimulate the interest of the parents and help them in determining which approach or approaches they should select to begin a study of their problems.

1. Why do pupils fail?
2. What do pupils do when they leave school?
3. What would a community be without a school?
4. Compare white collar jobs with the trades. Why are they both necessary?

5. Discuss what made the schools change their plans.
6. At what age do most pupils leave school?
7. How is education related to success in life?
8. What increasing family problems have you noticed?
9. What has technology to do with modern schools?
10. What are the uses of experiences in a child's life?
11. What value education?
12. What are educational costs?   Explain increases.

ACTIVITIES AND PROCEDURES

According to Hopkins[3] there are nine different kinds of activities which may be used in carrying through the unit of work.   In this particular unit, five are employed.   Whatever type of activity is adopted, care must be exercised to see that the activities bring into play the big and vital ideas which one wishes the parents to secure from the unit.   Other points to remember in selecting activities are:

1. Will the activities help to attain established objectives for the unit?
2. Are they of interest to parents?
3. Will they help carry out the aims of the Association?
4. Should they control the program of the Association?
5. Will they provide experiences to gain better understanding of the unit or topics to be considered?
6. Will they help parents secure proper concepts of the idea which is being developed in the unit?
7. Will they help parents to:
   a) Achieve the purposes of the Association?
   b) Attack problems independently?
   c) Interest more members?
   d) Help discover needs and solve problems.
   e) Secure greater coöperation?
   f) Increase the prestige of the Association by the effectiveness of its work?

A. Group Discussion Activities

1. Discuss the aims of education.   Define education.
2. Have a speaker talk on "The New Versus the Old School."   Have an exhibit of school work.
3. Discussion on education for worthy home membership.   How family ties have broken.   New problems of the school.
4. What industry demands of the new school.   Industrial and vocational schools.
5. The use of leisure and the new school.   The five-day week.
6. Economic demands.   Costs of education.   Education as an investment.

[3]The nine types are: 1. Orienting, 2. Building, 3. Research, 4. Group Discussion, 5. Creative Activities, 6. Appreciative, 7. Experimental, 8. Drill and Practice, 9. Culminating. Hopkins, L. Thomas. *Educational Method.* Vol. XI, October, 1931.   Page 7.

B. *Observation Activities*
  1. Teacher and class demonstration of courses of study.
  2. Visits to experimental schools.
  3. Exhibits of school work.
  4. Special activities in classroom.

C. *Research Activities*
  1. Study of needs by the membership.
  2. Study of new educational methods by a committee.
  3. Report of such committees.
  4. Report of research activities as carried on by National or State Congress.

D. *Orientation Activities*
  1. Report on the study of Association needs.
  2. Acquaintance with the problem—discussion.
  3. Committee report on possible attack or approach.

E. *Evaluation of Test of Unit*
  1. Is there an increase in attendance?
  2. Knowledge and interpretation of the school.
  3. Higher family standards.
  4. Does it facilitate acquaintance of teachers and parents?
  5. Coöperation in membership; in working out plans.
  6. Do outcomes attained satisfy needs? Are felt needs satisfied?
  7. Larger membership.
  8. Greater faith in education and school by parents.
  9. Objectives set up and realized.
  10. Member participation in Parent-Teacher Association work.
  11. Greater sense of responsibility toward child training.
  12. Knowledge of technique and devices used by schools.

MATERIALS TO BE USED

  1. Reports of Bicentennial Conference on Parent Education.
  2. Parent Education—National Congress of Parents and Teachers, Handbook.
  3. Reports of Lincoln School, New York City.
  4. Books on modern education:
     a) *Changing Civilization*, Kilpatrick.
     b) *Child-Centered School*, Rugg and Shumaker.
     c) *Middletown*, Lynd.
     d) *American Road to Culture*, Counts.
     e) *The Great Technology*, Rugg.
  5. Courses of study:
     a) Rugg's Social Studies Course.
     b) Lincoln School Units of Work.
     c) California State Plan of Parent Education.
     d) Plan of New College, Teachers College, Columbia University.
     e) National Education Association reports, etc.
     f) *Progressive Education Magazine*, Washington, D. C.

SUMMARY AND CONCLUSIONS

The program of the local Parent-Teacher Association determines the social significance of the organization, its attendance, and its membership. Since this is so, the program is deserving of more serious consideration than has been given to it in the past. That the present method of program-making is demonstrably unsatisfactory has been shown in the study of Association activity and results obtained and by the testimony of over one hundred Association presidents who experience difficulty in program-planning. The average program is formal and stereotyped, consisting of a number of unplanned and unrelated activities, whereas it should be conceived as an organized plan including the proper activities to meet the demands of the home, school, and community as well as to further the proposed functions and purposes of the organization.

It is in this connection that the unit of work system, now widely and successfully utilized in the schools of the United States, offers a solution to the problem of program-planning in the Parent-Teacher Association.

There is every reason to believe that the local Associations will improve their efficiency and increase their value to the community if they embark upon the plan suggested in this chapter. Their work will be more effective when they have analyzed and studied local needs and approached specific problems under the unit of work system. Such a unit will use all the energies of the membership in a concerted drive toward an accepted and definite objective. Its success depends in a large measure upon the setting up of the necessary objective, the adoption of a correct point of view, the right approach, and a careful selection of directed educational activities.

An experimental use of the unit of work system during the past year by the Parent-Teacher Association of the Woodrow Wilson School in Passaic, New Jersey, has resulted in a marked increase in the activity and efficiency of that group.

CHAPTER VIII

SUMMARY, CONCLUSIONS, AND RECOMMENDATIONS

Since its tentative beginnings as early as 1855, in the mothers' clubs and reading circles that grew up in connection with the first kindergartens, the movement for Parent-Teacher Association in all types of schools has grown until it has assumed an importance which makes it a factor to be reckoned with in a general consideration of educational policies in the United States. We find the Parent-Teacher Association diffused throughout the entire country, with an official national organization which alone numbers 1,511,203 individual members, while many other thousands of parents belong to independent organizations which carry on similar work but are not affiliated with the National Congress.

At its inception, the Mothers' Club was designed primarily to help its members learn more about the nature and nurture of the child; but as such organizations multiplied and spread into the elementary and high schools and as social conditions changed, for women especially, this primary purpose was lost sight of in the pressure of other interests of a more active kind. The diffusion of interests was such as to amount to a virtual abandonment of the principles of the founders, although these were still acknowledged and remained a latent force in the organization. The official national organization, the National Congress of Parents and Teachers, founded in 1897, did very little to check this diffusion of interests, and while working for extension of the Parent-Teacher movement did not formulate a constructive and unified program for its members which would have assisted and guided them to realize the potentialities inherent in the original conception. Consequently, the Association has not to this day fully developed its possibilities as a social force.

Meanwhile, however, the educators, who, on the whole, had been indifferent or hostile toward the Parent-Teacher Association, have under the influence of modern educational theory come to view it in a new light. Many of the most forward-looking among them

95

now regard it as a medium for the parent education which is vital to the success of the modern school. And many leaders of the Parent-Teacher Association are also realizing that this program of parent education represents the most fruitful contribution which the Association can make to the welfare of the child. As yet, however, there is no widespread reflection of these opinions of the educators and leaders in the work carried on by the rank and file of local Associations. Nor is there any concerted propaganda to bring about a re-orientation of program and activities which shall unify theory and lagging practice.

There would, therefore, seem to be necessary at this point a re-statement of principles and purposes in order that the aims of the organization might be achieved and its activities directed toward definite accomplishment. Furthermore, a relationship between school administration and Parent-Teacher Association needs to be established which will enable parents to be admitted to a legitimate participation in the educational process on one hand while on the other the school authorities can maintain their expert status. Only by a directed attempt to achieve this end can the Parent-Teacher Association justify its existence, its program, organization, and cost of maintenance.

As an existing organization within the limits of which much might be accomplished, the Parent-Teacher Association has a great potentiality of service. That its activities have unfortunately been misdirected to a very great extent impairs the immediate value of its work but does not impair the potential value.

Any study, such as this one undertaken by the author, will inevitably reveal to the impartial observer serious but remediable defects. Since this is true, the author here presents a list of specific recommendations by which the efficiency and value of the Parent-Teacher Association work may be increased.

RECOMMENDATIONS

Undoubtedly the most serious single factor which has militated against the success of the Parent-Teacher Association has been its wide diffusion of interest, its inability to understand that its purpose and function, in fact its only excuse for existence, is its potentiality as a means of educating parents in order to make those parents realize their job and understand their duties to the child and to the community. Too often entertainments, social intercourse, and unrelated program activities have comprised the plan of work outlined by the local Associations to the virtual exclusion of worthwhile educational material and activities. There would, therefore, seem to be a discrepancy between the theoretical understanding of purposes and the activities in which the Associations are actually engaged. The primary recommendations are, therefore:

I. That a direct relationship be established between the activities and the theoretical understanding of functions and admitted purposes of the Parent-Teacher Association. Since 20,000 units affiliated with the National Congress look to it for leadership in defining purpose and suggesting activities, and since its prestige among these groups is great, the following suggestions are made with respect to the National Congress:

A. That the National Congress join with educators in an effort to clarify its statements of theoretical functions to be presented to its member Associations, together with an outline of activities which would assist the member Associations to embark upon a complete reorganization of their programs. This would necessitate the abandonment of all unrelated interests and a clear recognition that the purpose of the movement can never be realized through a program of random activities with only a tenuous relation to function.

B. That the National Congress, in presenting such an outline of functions and activities, provide for sufficient elasticity and flexibility of program to permit local Associations to care for their own particular problems.

C. That the National Congress require local units to make the unrelated activities of a program subservient to a unified program of parent education. Thus, standards for admission to the National Congress should include a carefully organized plan of program activity which shows an understanding of proposed aims and functions and relates activities to these.

II. That an authoritative educational body (such as the Department of Superintendence of the National Education Association) appoint a committee to analyze and define the strictly professional aspects of educational practice which it regards as the special province of the school and to study further the relationship which should exist between the administrative authorities and the Parent-Teacher Association. This should also include the specific functions which concern both groups and which show the mutual interdependence of the two groups. The deliberations and recommendations of this committee should be widely circulated among educators to serve the purpose of clarifying much of the confusion which now exists on these two points. It is suggested in connection with this recommendation that representatives of parents' associations be given an opportunity to sit with the committee.

III. That such authoritative agencies as the various universities and teachers colleges take the initiative in providing for the careful training of leaders by means of institutes and definite courses, both credit and non-credit. The National Congress could be asked to coöperate with these institutions. The research and study of these trained leaders will help the local units to consolidate their activities and move forward with a carefully planned and unified program.

IV. That further experimentation with the unit of work system described in this study as a method of program planning be carried on. Under this system an Association must determine what, in respect to general aims and purposes, are its greatest problems. It must then select activities relating to these problems which shall engage the interest and activity of the entire Association over a specified length of time. In this way the program may be consolidated into a series of worthwhile experiences under a central idea or "unit."

V. That Associations continue to be self-supporting. This should not, however, prevent the local educational system from assisting the work of the Parent-Teacher Association in any way possible, once the policy of self-support has been established.

VI. That the Associations be given definite status in the boards of education by-laws, which should define their rights. This is required for stability and prestige. The Associations should remain independent, organized voluntarily by interested parents, and should exercise no legal control over the schools.

VII. That an efficient publicity program be set up under the direction of leaders trained by state associations or other centralized agencies responsible for general organization and administration, and that these give considerable time to a study of more efficient means of arousing the interest of the public and the members.

VIII. That the Associations take a definite stand in helping to solve educational problems. They must acquire social power not only by discussing the fundamental factors in education but by taking appropriate action when the education of the child is at stake. Giving of constructive help when school budgets are slashed and effective protest against political interference with the schools are two examples of opportunities for action open to them which are definitely related to their primary objective.

IX. That Associations take as their goal a representative membership from the community, large and broad enough to typify the thinking and philosophy of the particular locality and to insure that representative policies and procedures receive the approval and sanction of the district.

X. That the Parent-Teacher Association refrain from making decisions in those provinces which are highly professional and therefore strictly belong to the school. This does not mean that the Association should not familiarize itself with the work and philosophy of the school.

XI. That school administrators recognize their responsibility in educating parents in regard to the school's work and procedure. Not until the educator with zeal and interest is willing to guide parents into channels of proper activity and to interpret to them modern education will the Parent-Teacher Association accomplish the purposes for which it is organized.

XII. That the teaching force of the school recognize its responsibility to contribute actively in every way possible toward the furtherance of the aims of the Parent-Teacher Association.

XIII. That wider use be made of the device of planning the business procedure of the meeting through the executive committee. Business and entertainment features should be subordinated to the educational part of the meeting.

XIV. That wider use be made of the device of organizing study groups within the Parent-Teacher Association to pursue intensive study, under the direction of competent authorities, of problems based on the needs and interests of these smaller groups.

XV. That all financial and business transactions of the Associations be based on a sound accounting procedure.

XVI. That the Parent-Teacher Associations and parents' associations operating independently of the National Congress be subjected to careful study in the very near future. These are so numerous and present so many opportunities for local experimentation that they would undoubtedly yield much valuable information. For example, the United Parents Association of New York City has made a unique and invaluable contribution to the whole movement both in analyzing aims, functions, and purposes, and in devising new methods of organization and community coöperation.

XVII. That the turnover of membership be studied further. This problem has not received adequate attention. Careful study of it should yield information regarding the stability of these local units and the extent of the influence they actually exercise.

BIBLIOGRAPHY*

BUTTERWORTH, J. E. *The Parent-Teacher Association and Its Work.* New York, Macmillan Company, 1928.

*Note: Appendix C of this book by Dr. Butterworth (pp. 137-41) includes a list of selected unannotated references which consider the work of the Parent-Teacher Association and various aspects of education particularly useful to parents and teachers.

From the date of this bibliography materials and references which have to do with the work of the Parent-Teacher Association may be found in the following sources:

1. Education Index. A cumulative author and subject index to a selected list of educational periodicals, books, and pamphlets. H. W. Wilson Co., New York.
2. United States Office of Education, Department of the Interior, Washington, D. C. Gives out data regarding literature developed in Parent-Teacher Association work.
3. National Congress of Parents and Teachers, 1201 Sixteenth Street, N. W., Washington, D. C. Prepares periodically a list of books helpful to the parent and teacher.

In gathering material for this study reference was made to the following books, reports, and magazine articles:

THE WORK OF THE PARENT-TEACHER ASSOCIATION

BUTTERWORTH, JULIAN E. *The Parent-Teacher Association.* New York, Macmillan Company, 1928.

GOLDEN, MRS. EMMA. *Study of Parent-Teacher Associations in North Dakota.* University of Minnesota, 1928.

INTERNATIONAL BUREAU OF EDUCATION. *Coöperation of School and Home.* Geneva. Rue des Maraichers 44, Geneva, Switzerland, 1929.

MASON, MARTHA SPRAGUE. *Parents and Teachers.* New York, Ginn and Company, 1928.

MCANDREW, WILLIAM M. "Parent Teachers Getting Formidable." *School and Society,* Vol. 29, June 1929, pp. 712-22.

METTEN, J. A. *Survey of the Work of Local Parent-Teacher Associations of Ohio During the School Year 1928-1929.* Ohio State University (M. A. Thesis), 1930.

MOEHLMANN, A. B. "Defining Rights and Duties of Parent-Teacher Associations. *Nation's Schools,* Vol. 7, June 1931, pp. 55-59.

NATIONAL CONGRESS OF PARENTS AND TEACHERS. *Handbook.* Washington, D. C., 1931.

NATIONAL CONGRESS OF PARENTS AND TEACHERS. *Proceedings for 1928-1932.* Washington, D. C., 1932.

NATIONAL CONGRESS OF PARENTS AND TEACHERS. *Through the Years.* Washington, D. C., 1930.

"New Force in Education." *Proceedings of Conference* Held at Teachers College under auspices of National Congress of Parents and Teachers and Teachers College, December 5th and 6th, 1929.

REEVE, MARGARET W., AND LOMBARD, ELLEN C. *The Parent-Teacher Associations, 1924–1926.* Bulletin, U. S. Bureau of Education, 1927. No. II.

REEVE, M. W. "Countries in All Parts of the World Are Coöperating to Bring Together Home and School." *School Life,* Vol. 15, No. 5, November 1929.

ROGERS, MARIA L. *A Contribution to the Theory and Practice of Parents and Teachers.* New York, United Parents Association, 1931.

State School Improvement Associations. Rural School Pamphlet No. 42, U. S. Bureau of Education, Washington, D. C., 1927.

WATKINS, FLORENCE V. "Courses in Parent-Teacher Association Work." *School and Society,* Vol. 9, May 11, 1929, pp. 599–602.

MATERIALS ON VARIOUS ASPECTS OF EDUCATION WHICH ARE PARTICULARLY USEFUL TO PARENTS AND TEACHERS INTERESTED IN PARENT-TEACHER ASSOCIATION WORK

BRUNER, H. B. *South Dakota Course of Study.* Department of Instruction, Department of Curriculum Revision, Pierre, South Dakota, 1930.

FARLEY, BELMONT. *What to Tell the Public About Our Schools.* Bureau of Publications, Teachers College, Columbia University, New York City, 1929.

HOPKINS, L. T. "Creative Education." *Educational Method,* Vol. 9, October 1931, pp. 1-8.

HART, JOSEPH K. *Adult Education.* New York, Thomas Y. Crowell Co., 1927.

LINDEMAN, E. C. "Sociological Aspects of Parent Education." *Journal of Educational Sociology,* Vol. 5, April 1932, pp. 500-07.

MOEHLMANN, A. B. *Public School Relations.* New York, Rand McNally Company, 1928.

NEWLON, JESSE H. Paper on "Parent Education," presented at Biennial Conference of National Council of Parent Education. Washington, D. C., November 1930.

REYNOLDS, ROLLO G. *Newspaper Publicity for the Public Schools.* New York, A. G. Seiler, 1922.

APPENDIX

Tables and Charts
Outline, Rating Scale, and Questionnaire

TABLE A

NUMBER OF INDEPENDENT PARENT-TEACHER ASSOCIATIONS AS REPORTED
FROM THE STATE OFFICES OF BRANCHES OF THE NATIONAL
CONGRESS OF PARENTS AND TEACHERS IN 1932

(No Data from States Not Listed)

Maryland	393		Nebraska	50
Alabama	350		Tennessee	50
Georgia	250		Washington	50
Vermont	200		West Virginia	50
Arkansas	200		Colorado	50
Illinois	193		Delaware	10
Iowa	192		Idaho	10
Louisiana	100		Maine	10
South Dakota	100		D. C.	6
Oklahoma	100		Wyoming	6
Virginia	80		New Mexico	5
			Hawaii	1
South Carolina - Many (S.I.A.)				

TABLE B

DISTRIBUTION OF 20,072 LOCAL UNITS OF THE NATIONAL CONGRESS OF
PARENT-TEACHER ASSOCIATIONS AMONG DIFFERENT TYPES OF SCHOOLS

Grade School	18,427
Senior High School	722*
Junior High School	433*
Pre-School	308
Parochial School	91
Senior College	23
Kindergarten	17
Church	15
Junior College	7
Private	7
Other	22

*The Junior-Senior High School Associations form only about $\frac{1}{25}$ of the units but have nearly $\frac{1}{15}$ of the members.

105

TABLE C

THE NUMBER OF ACTIVITIES CARRIED ON IN THE VARIOUS STATES FOR THE
YEARS 1929, 1930, 1931, AS REPORTED BY THE PRESIDENT OF THE STATE
CONGRESS

*The rank given indicates the number of times the activity was mentioned by the
President of the State Congress*

ACTIVITY	FREQUENCY OF OCCURRENCE	ACTIVITY	FREQUENCY OF OCCURRENCE
Summer Round-Up (Correcting Physical Defects)..............	104	Beautification of School	9
		Physical Education...	8
Bulletins..............	100	Kindergarten Education..............	8
Publicity.............	91	Illiteracy...........	8
Founders' Day........	76	Character Education..	8
Child Health..........	68	Leisure (Use of Leisure	
Parent Education......	64	Time).............	8
Radio................	52	Handicapped Children	7
Courses..............	50	Art.................	6
Libraries.............	48	Reading Rooms......	6
Study Groups........	42	Americanization......	6
Legislation...........	37	Pageants...........	5
Citizenship...........	36	Correspondence Courses	4
Music...............	34	Scrap-Books.........	4
Safety Education......	31	Colored Education...	4
School Banking (Thrift)	30	Poster Contest.......	4
Juvenile Protection.....	26	Baby Clinic..........	4
Motion Pictures.......	25	Lectures.............	4
Home Education.......	25	Supply Textbooks....	3
Rural Education.......	23	Vocational Education.	3
Humane Education....	18	Farm Bureau........	3
Home Economics......	18	Community Development.............	3
Scholarship Fund......	18	Free Clinics..........	2
Social Hygiene........	17	Church Associations..	2
Mental Hygiene.......	16	Bands..............	2
Recreation...........	14	Visual Education.....	2
Playgrounds..........	13	Dental Education....	2
Spiritual Training......	12	Guidance...........	2
Leadership...........	12	Holidays...........	1
Nutrition.............	10	Clothes Conservation.	1
Exhibits.............	9	Narcotic Education...	1
		Nursing............	1

*The above table includes only activities reported by State Officials, from *Proceedings* of
National Congress of Parents and Teachers, "President's Reports," 1929, 1930, 1931. Washington, D. C.

TABLE D

How 100 Parent-Teacher Associations Raise Their Funds*, in Order of Frequency

Entertainments, Movies, etc.	44
Card Parties	20
Sales (food, candy, clothing, etc.)	19
Dramatics, Operettas	17
Dinners	13
Carnivals or Bazaars	10
Subscriptions or Donations, Gifts	8
Lectures	7
Dances	5
Athletics	5
Community Projects	5
Theater Parties	4
Finance Committee	2
Miscellaneous	2

*Dues, not included above, are means of support of every association.

TABLE E

Proportional Distribution of Income, as to Source, of National Congress

Dues per member 5¢	81 %
National Life Membership	16 %
State Life Membership	1.5%
Delinquent Dues	.5%
Other Gifts	.3%
Miscellaneous	.1%

TABLE F

How 100 Associations Spend Their Money, in Order of Frequency

Equipment, Playgrounds, Books, Pictures, and Radios	55	
Refreshments	40	
Child Welfare, Relief (General Welfare)	35*	
Student Aid	20	
Dues, State and National	20	
Speakers	19	
Convention, Delegates, etc.	18	
Study Groups	17	
Clinics (Health)	15	
Parental Education	15	
Paid Lectures	14	
Charities	12	
Stationery, Printing, etc.	12	
Under-privileged Children, nutrition, lunch room, etc.	10	
Banquets, Teacher Receptions	10	
Prizes	9	
Rent of Meeting Places	6	
Publicity and Publications	4	
School Band	3	
Athletics	3	
Libraries	3	
Parties	3	
Boy and Girl Camps	2	

*This item is on the increase. The economic condition of the country has given an impetus to the spending of money by the Association for relief.

TABLE G

DISTRIBUTION OF EXPENDITURES OF THE NATIONAL CONGRESS

Presidents' Fund..	$ 3,554.14
Summer Round-up...	4,200.00
Administration Fund..	3,641.20
Officers' Departments' & Committees' Expenses.............	894.02
National Office..	11,769.07
Salaries...	40,396.35
International Federation of Home & School.................	1,000.00
Convention—Denver, Colorado..............................	3,115.55
Auditor National Office....................................	100.00
Auditor & Bond Treasurer..................................	175.00
Treasurer's Expense including clerical help................	500.00
Traveling Expenses—Executive Committee..................	7,379.39
Exhibits (Outside)	257.73
Stationery...	470.75
Publications...	18,748.04
Equipment...	1,892.92
Field..	7,902.47
Royalty "Parents & Teachers" to Endowment Fund.........	174.15
Endowment Fund—National & State Life Memberships......	2,431.90
Emblems...	5,951.00
Balance 1929–30 Administration...........................	561.52
President's Fund Revolving—Additional....................	300.00
National Office Revolving—Additional.....................	300.00
Convention, 1931, Hot Springs, Ark.......................	46.91
Miscellaneous..	327.43
TOTAL...	**$116,089.54**

TABLE H

A Measuring Scale for Parent–Teacher Associations*
(ShowingWeighted Judgments of 75 Jurors)

Items	Total Score Allotted	Distribu- tion of Scores
I. Programs and Activities		
A. Preliminary meeting of the executive committee for making general plans............	5	5
B. Methods of planning programs and activities.	5	
1. Definite study of educational needs......		3
2. Preparation of programs early in the year.		1
3. Focusing of programs upon relatively few needs.................................		1
C. The year's objectives and their attainment...	11	
1. Giving members an understanding of the objectives and methods of the school......		3
2. Teaching members to apply accepted educational objectives and methods to the out-of-school environment..................		2
3. Facilitating acquaintance among parents and teachers.........................		2
4. Aiding in educating the community to desirable aspects of the school's program....		2
5. Raising funds under certain conditions....		1
6. Under certain conditions giving to the school officials judgment as to where the school fails or succeeds.................		1
D. Maintaining a reasonable balance between entertainment and non-entertainment features	2	2
E. Reasonable adherence to educational problems of children as contrasted with general community problems...........................	2	2
F. Non-interference with work of board or teaching staff...............................	2	2
G. Percentage total membership utilized during the year in some way.....................	2	2
H. Extension work, such as work in unorganized territory; collecting funds; Founders' Day....	1	1
Total................................	30	30
II. Administration		
A. Committee organization...................	4	4
B. Financial policies.......................	4	
1. Preparation of budget early in year.......		1
2. Budget in keeping with educational program		2
3. Reasonable adherence to this budget......		1
C. Promptness in attending to state and national business...............................	1	1
D. Dignified publicity of parent-teacher matters.	4	4

Items	Total Score Allotted	Distribution of Scores
E. Sending delegates to state and district conventions....................................	1	1
F. Absence of friction and prevalence of spirit of coöperation among members................	3	3
G. Meetings.................................	3	
1. Frequency—(number that can be held successfully).........................		1
2. Regularity—(each month according to schedule).............................		2
Total...............................	20	20
III. Membership and Attendance		
A. Per cent of parents who are members........	3	3
B. Per cent of men members..................	3	3
C. Per cent of teachers who are members.......	3	3
D. Per cent of membership in average attendance	3	3
E. Per cent of teachers in average attendance...	3	3
Total.................................	15	15
IV. Program of Parent Education		
A. Preliminary study of problem...............	3	3
B. Focusing program on needs.................	3	3
C. Organization............................	6	6
D. Study groups	8	
1. Classification of interests.................		2
2. Leadership............................		4
3. Subjects or material covered.............		1
4. Financial support of board of education...		1
Total.................................	20	20
V. Health:		
Summer Round-Up (location and means for correcting physical and mental defects of children)..	8	
A. Discovering of defects.....................		2
B. Organization and procedure; set-up and plan.		2
C. Results or accomplishments; actual number of defects corrected as a result of Parent-Teacher Association leadership..............		4
VI. Effectiveness in bringing about changes for the better in regard to child development; social adjustment in and out of school; school housing; better teaching; better community attitude, etc...............................	7	7
Total.................................	15	15
Grand Total...........................		100

*Adapted from Butterworth's Self Measuring Scale for Parent-Teacher Associations. (*The Parent-Teacher Association*, Butterworth, J. E. Macmillan Co., 1928.)

CHART A

EXAMPLE OF THE ORGANIZATION OF A STATE BRANCH OF THE NATIONAL
CONGRESS OF PARENTS AND TEACHERS

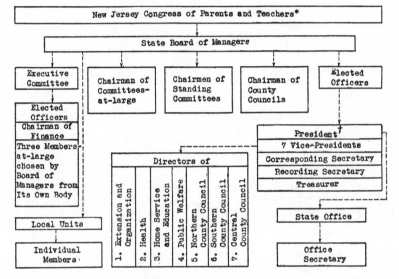

*Notes: 1. The Convention is the policy forming group of the Congress. The Board of
Managers carries out the policies and conducts the business of the Congress between
Conventions.

2. The State Congress elects its own officers, adopts its own by-laws and legislates for its
local units. State by-laws and standing rules of a State branch must be in harmony
with those in the National Congress.

3. States vary in their organization. The above is an example of one type of organization.
Some states are divided into districts for purposes of administration. In some states
large cities having school systems separate from the county school system, organize city
councils to unify the work in the city.

†The presidents of the state branches are members of the Board of Managers of the National
Congress of Parents and Teachers.

CHART B

RELATION OF NATIONAL COMMITTEES TO STATE, DISTRICT,
COUNCIL, AND LOCAL UNITS

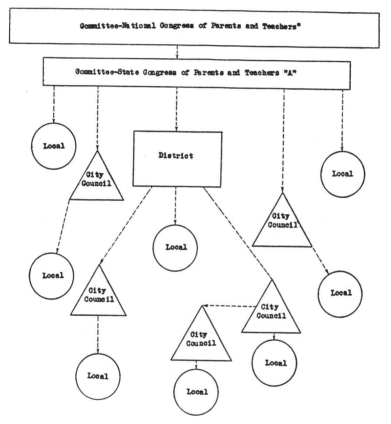

Chart shows through which channels various committees work. Where the city is large, the county council is omitted occasionally, but most often it is retained because the city has a city Superintendent and the county a County Superintendent and the two systems work independently. "A" Most frequent course.

*Prepared by the National Congress of Parents and Teachers, Washington, D. C.

CHART C

ORGANIZATION OF NATIONAL CONGRESS (1930)

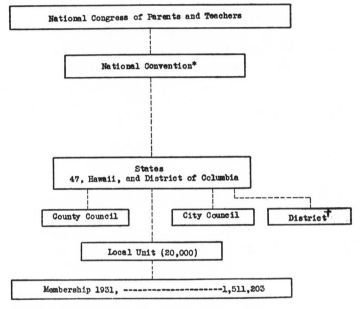

National Congress of Parents and Teachers

National Convention*

| States |
| 47, Hawaii, and District of Columbia |

County Council	City Council	District†

Local Unit (20,000)

Membership 1931, --------------------1,511,203

*Convention is included in chart because of its power as a policy forming group.
†District is used in some states to divide state into smaller units.

CHART D

RELATION OF THE PARENT-TEACHER ASSOCIATION TO EDUCATIONAL SYSTEM

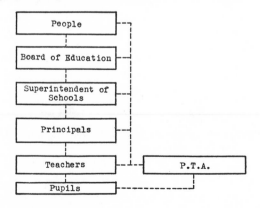

People
Board of Education
Superintendent of Schools
Principals
Teachers
Pupils

P.T.A.

CHART E

Governing Bodies of National Congress of Parents and Teachers

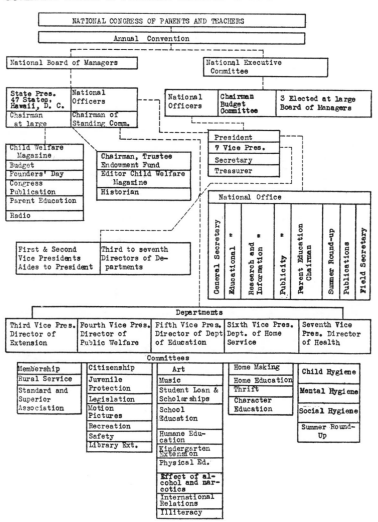

CHART F

DUTIES OF MEMBERS IN THE PARENT-TEACHER ASSOCIATION

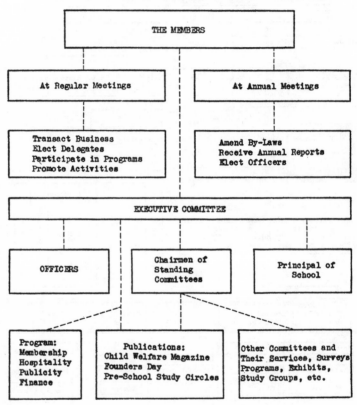

THE MEMBERS

At Regular Meetings

At Annual Meetings

Transact Business
Elect Delegates
Participate in Programs
Promote Activities

Amend By-Laws
Receive Annual Reports
Elect Officers

EXECUTIVE COMMITTEE

OFFICERS

Chairmen of
Standing
Committees

Principal of
School

Program:
Membership
Hospitality
Publicity
Finance

Publications:
Child Welfare Magazine
Founders Day
Pre-School Study Circles

Other Committees and
Their Services, Surveys
Programs, Exhibits,
Study Groups, etc.

AN OUTLINE OF A GOOD PROJECT IN STUDY GROUPS

A YEAR'S PLAN FOR STUDY GROUPS AS SUGGESTED BY THE LINCOLN SCHOOL PARENT-TEACHER ASSOCIATION, NEW YORK CITY

I. GRADE GROUP MEETINGS

Parents of every grade to meet in October and again in the spring to discuss with teachers the work of the grade and plan for closer coöperation.

One of these grade meetings to be an *evening* meeting, so fathers can meet with teachers. (Several grades could meet on the same evening to make it easier for the teachers.)

These Grade Meetings to (1) be arranged for by grade representatives; (2) have programs planned by grade representatives working with teacher, in coöperation with the trained leader; (3) be presided over by grade representative.

Aim for 100 per cent attendance at these two meetings of each grade group. Other grade meetings could be called by the teacher when desired. Grade representatives would assist teacher in getting group together.

Any teacher or any parent could suggest matters which she would like to have discussed at these meetings; but these suggestions would be made in advance, and through the grade representatives.

Grade representatives chosen by parents in grades.

Several preliminary meetings of grade representatives for discussion of technique in leading meetings.

II. SEVERAL ELECTIVE STUDY GROUPS

Make out a course of study covering the large topics in each series, with a two- or three-year sequence, so that parents can look ahead and plan their work.

Allow flexibility in this program, with some meetings to be devoted to particular needs of the group; e.g.:

Group 1. The Physical and Psychological Development of the Young Child.

Group 2. The Physical and Psychological Development of the Pre-Adolescent.

Group 3. The Physical and Psychological Development of the Adolescent.

Groups 1 to 3: Led by professional leader. Assigned readings bringing parents up to date on scientific findings on the subject. Experts brought in as needed. Parent participation encouraged, but leader carrying responsibility of planning and leading discussion.

Group 4. One series each year on some study of social significance. Talks by experts or persons of experience in social work. Also a laboratory project, such as providing a recreation club for boys of neighborhood who now constitute a social problem for the school.

Group 5. One "seminar" group where parents themselves contribute from their own study and experience. Selected specific topics, useful to parents of any age child, such as: "Training Children in the Use of Money." (Parents taking this course would expect to assume much responsibility for making it a success; they would read; prepare material to present to the others; etc.) Some of the contributions of this group would be used in Groups 1 to 3.   Grade representatives would be encouraged to join this group.

DEFINITION OF STUDY GROUPS WITH RECOMMENDATIONS

"Study Groups" may be defined as a number of smaller groups of parents of the regular membership meeting to discuss problems of interest in an intimate way.   Objectives of such groups may be:

1. To facilitate acquaintanceship and stimulate coöperative effort among parents.

2. To provide for the particular interest of parents.

3. To give the parent the responsibility of planning and contributing to the project or problem.

4. To give parents a greater insight into the problems of the school and home.

5. To give parents a better understanding of their function as parents.

6. To contribute or pass on well thought out "findings" and results to other groups.

7. To discover potential leaders.

RECOMMENDATIONS FOR STUDY GROUPS

1. Organize study groups according to grades.   Have a grade representative responsible to develop plans and programs.   Teacher should be relieved of details and planning.

2. Initiating study groups needs careful planning and organization to give leaders understanding and skill to carry out plans and to develop an interest and understanding on the part of the groups in the idea and in the plans.

3. An attempt should be made to find a unity of interest.   Parents should be made conscious that there are problems common to most of the group which can be considered by all with profit.

4. Teachers should be included in the plans and work of the Study Group.

5. Both the expert and local talent should be used to solve its problems.

6. Include whole membership.   Plan definite "tie-up" between all study groups and with the larger general meetings of the Association.   Someone should be delegated with this responsibility.

7. Lay leaders are necessary to secure desirable results but they must have opportunity for training in leadership.

8. Several types of study groups should be set up to provide for the various interests of the groups.

9. Parents must be given the opportunity to indicate their preference in regard to the topics to be considered and opportunity to participate to the fullest extent in all meetings.

SUMMER ROUND-UP OF NATIONAL CONGRESS

1930 Accomplishment

I. PARTICIPATION OF PARENT-TEACHER ASSOCIATIONS IN SUMMER ROUND-UP, 1930.

	NUMBER OF PARENT-TEACHER ASSOCIATION UNITS		
	Registering	Carrying Through	% Completing Work
States represented...............	43	43	100
Communities represented.........	1,880	761	40.4
City Groups represented..........	2,386	1,358	50.5
Town Groups represented.........	1,065	317	29.7
Rural Groups represented.........	812	244	30.0
TOTAL.....................	4,563	1,919	42.0

II. PHYSICAL DEFECTS DISCOVERED AND CORRECTED IN SUMMER ROUND-UP, 1930.

	NUMBER OF DEFECTS		
	Discovered	Corrected	Per Cent Corrected
Eyes..........................	3,094	946	30.5
Ears..........................	1,830	558	30.4
Teeth.........................	29,850	9,135	30.6
Tonsils........................	21,179	4,821	22.7
Adenoids......................	12,402	2,825	22.7
Nose..........................	1,636	387	23.6
Heart.........................	1,347	309	22.9
Glands........................	7,644	1,580	20.6
Lungs.........................	786	225	28.6
Posture.......................	3,885	703	18.0
Feet..........................	2,722	554	20.3
Underweight...................	10,196	3,658	35.8
Skin..........................	1,152	467	40.5
Hernia........................	675	127	18.8
Abdomen......................	914	174	19.0
Circumcision...................	3,128	558	17.8
Miscellaneous..................	3,292	1,478	44.8
TOTAL.....................	105,732	28,505	26.9

III. NUMBER OF CHILDREN RECEIVING IMMUNIZATION AGAINST:
Smallpox....................18,872
Diphtheria................... 9,908
Typhoid..................... 1,221

IV. NUMBER OF CHILDREN ENTERING SCHOOL (KINDERGARTEN
OR FIRST GRADE), FALL, 1930.............................102,490
NUMBER OF THESE CHILDREN RECEIVING ROUND-UP EXAMINA-
TION.. 55,526
NUMBER OF PARENTS OR GUARDIANS PRESENT AT EXAMINATION 37,965

V. NUMBER OF THESE UNITS WHICH MET NATIONAL CAMPAIGN
REQUIREMENTS AND RECEIVED THE CERTIFICATE AWARD..... 1,462

COPY OF SCALE RATING IMPORTANT OBJECTIVES OF THE
PARENT-TEACHER ASSOCIATION
AS RANKED BY 40 ASSOCIATION PRESIDENTS AND 40 SCHOOL ADMINISTRATORS
(See Table 1, page 50)

The following list of objectives of Parents or Parent-Teacher Associations
has been assembled by compiling all of the objectives suggested as desirable
by educators, experts, and officials in the field of P.T.A. work, such as state
and local presidents.

Assuming a typical association, will you rank these in the order of importance which in your judgment they should assume in the Association's program? No. 1 means that you feel the objective so ranked is most important,
and No. 2 means that which should be the next concern of the Association.
A rank of 17 indicates the objective which in your judgment should receive the
least attention of the list there given.

The list is made in random order and does not indicate the author's preference.

RANK
ORDER

1. Making material gifts to the school, such as pictures, radios, various
   kinds of equipment, not provided by the school board.   ——

2. Financing experimental work in the school curriculum, to be used
   as demonstrations, with the expectation that they will later be taken
   over by the school board. Such activities in the past have included open-air classes, milk for undernourished children, school
   orchestras, etc.   ——

3. Providing general knowledge of the school philosophy, curriculum
   making in relation to the changing social situation, teaching methods and their purpose, school procedures, such as ungraded classes,
   psychological testing, etc., for membership and community.   ——

4. Providing information to bring about changes for the better in
   regard to child development, habits of learning, social adjustment
   in and out of school, training methods to be used in the home, attitudes towards choice of a vocation, etc.—now generally summed
   up under the phrase, "parent education."   ——

5. Providing a cultural program with no necessary emphasis on the
   needs of the child, such as musical concerts, lectures on non-
   professional subjects, dramatics, entertainments, etc.   ——

6. Providing charitable relief for families of poor in the school district;
   providing glasses and shoes, etc., for needy children.   ——

7. Providing scholarships for gifted children.   ——

8. Working on a legislative program for better school conditions, new
   schools, new playgrounds, playground equipment, increases in
   school budget, defense against unnecessary attack of public school
   expenditures.   ——

9. Providing an understanding of the parents' role in modern education, the value and opportunities of the P.T.A., of the social responbilities of parenthood, of parent-child relationship. This sociological material to be presented through inspirational lectures. ——

10. Organizing and assisting study groups in child development, the parent-child relationship, generally known as "parent education." This objective differs from No. 4 in that it involves *intensive* study of bibliography, case-histories, etc. Under the guidance of a professional or intelligent lay-leader with adequate equipment. No. 4 assumes only that such material will be presented in lecture or discussion form in so far as practicable at the large meetings of the Association. ——

11. Coöperating with the educational staff of the school to solve certain school problems, such as: homework, reading habits, ill-considered complaints, mistakes occurring through misunderstanding, lack of friendly relations between teachers and parents. ——

12. Providing a means for social intercourse between parents and teachers for the purpose of facilitating acquaintance and building a partnership between home and school. ——

13. Helping toward a better understanding of community conditions, community needs and a community program for child and civic welfare. This would have to be done in coöperation with other civic and social organizations. ——

14. Working to correct physical defects of children through such devices as the "Summer Round Up" or others aimed to prepare children for entering school without physical defects; to insure better use of existing recreational opportunities; better use of leisure time. ——

15. Supporting state and national organizations in their efforts for equalization of educational opportunities throughout the several states, for nation-wide reform for favorable legislation for adequate schools and citizenship. ——

16. Educating the public as to the Association's program with the idea of securing public support for the advancement of that program. Making extensive use of a publicity set-up. ——

COPY OF CHECK LIST USED TO ANALYZE THE WORK OF
THE TEN CASE STUDIES

Analysis of............................Parent-Teacher Association
Located at...............................
Signed...................................
Write fully:
  1. Age of Association
  2. Size of Association
  3. Regular meetings per year
  4. Special meetings per year
  5. How and why formed? (History)
  6. Organization (Personnel) All working?—Coöperative? Committee plans, etc. (Method of work)
  7. Per cent of attendance at meetings?
  8. Per cent of teachers belonging?
  9. Per cent of men belonging?
 10. Per cent of homes represented?
 11. Does a study of needs determine activities? Ability of personnel to select important activities?
 12. Type of activities:
      a) Educational?
      b) Number
      c) Relation to needs
      d) Do they solve your problems?
 13. Do you have printed programs?
 14. Is budget related to activities?
 15. How is money expended? (Financial policy)
 16. Is there coöperation between all groups?
      a) Any friction? Ever?
 17. Wider Outlook affiliated with:
      a) Council
      b) State
      c) National
 18. Business procedure: sound accounting—expenses audited?
 19. Philosophy behind organization. Attitude toward progressive Education unselfish? etc.
 20. Is there a real publicity program? Any publications?
 21. What is reaction of school?
 22. What is reaction of Community? Effect of P.T.A. on Community?
 23. Attitude toward lay and professional functions? P.T.A. keep within its province?
 24. How Association works? Study groups. One leader only. Delegate duties, etc.
 25. Any help from higher authoritative bodies? National Body, higher council, etc.?

26. Help from study and research furnished by school system, State or National Association?
27. Can you boast of real leadership in your association? Ones who know and take the lead?
28. Program meeting needs? Is there a balance between Entertainment, Social, Educational, etc.
29. Is program unified? All energies directed toward one big job?
30. Does P.T.A. institute reforms such as:
    a) Legislation
    b) City reform
    c) School support
       1) new education
    d) Teachers
       1) salaries
       2) tenure
       3) pension, etc.
       4) welfare

31. Aggressive
    a) To dictate policies of Board or School?
    b) To support education and Child Welfare?
    c) Assumes a place in body politic? Dynamic?
32. Is interest of members real and unselfish, trying to do worth while things?
33. Do many members drop out? Any record of *turnover?* Do kindergarten parents remain members until child graduates?
34. Independent in thought and action?
35. Has Association ever been political?
36. Enumerate major difficulties.
37. Does your plan provide for *Education of parents along such lines as:* (a) new education demanded by changes in Society; (b) what the schools are doing to meet these changes; (c) objectives of education, etc.
38. How are leaders trained?
    a) Professional courses (college, etc.)
    b) Study groups
    c) Instruction from National Headquarters or Central Organization?
    d) Self-trained?
39. List desirable changes brought about conclusively by work of P.T.A.

a) Parent education or enlightenment.	h) Study of supplies
b) Teachers more friendly	i) Fewer complaints
c) Parents more interested in school	j)
d) Health program	k)
e) Playgrounds	l)
f) Boys clubs	m)
g) Equipment	n)

Write in other means by which you would check an Association for efficiency (explain things as fully as you can)

Remarks:

LETTER SENT TO 100 PRESIDENTS OF LOCAL PARENT-TEACHER
ASSOCIATIONS AND 100 SCHOOL ADMINISTRATORS

Dear President:

Please rank in order of importance (1-11) the activities which you and your
Association consider in carrying out your program of work.   Mark 1 for the
most important, 2 for the next, etc.   A mark of 11 will indicate the activity
to which you attach the least significance of the 11 listed activities.   The order
here given is a random one.*

1. Study Groups**
2. Demonstrations of School Work.
3. Program of Parent Education.
4. Study of School Work and Methods.
5. Community Projects.
6. Making Gifts to School.
7. Social Intercourse.
8. Entertainments.
9. Study of Child Psychology.
10. Publicity.
11. Helping to Solve School Problems.

Very truly yours,

STATES FROM WHICH QUESTIONNAIRES WERE RECEIVED

New Jersey	10	Rhode Island	2
Pennsylvania	8	South Carolina	2
California	7	Virginia	2
Colorado	7	Wyoming	2
Louisiana	6	Arkansas	1
New York	6	Delaware	1
Connecticut	5	Florida	1
Illinois	4	Georgia	1
Ohio	4	Indiana	1
Alabama	3	Maine	1
Massachusetts	3	Mississippi	1
Minnesota	3	Missouri	1
Wisconsin	3	New Hampshire	1
Kansas	2	Texas	1
Michigan	2	Vermont	1
North Carolina	2		
North Dakota	2	TOTAL	98
Oklahoma	2		

*Child Welfare listed by some of the Associations in the field was not included because of its
broad concept and because of its inclusion in the eleven activities above.

**Includes Child Development, Parent-Child Relationship, School Methods, Psychology, etc.

PARENT-TEACHER ASSOCIATIONS USED FOR CASE STUDIES

The ten Parent-Teacher Associations used for case studies were selected from the following cities:

Bridgeport, Connecticut
Fairfield, Connecticut
Greenwich, Connecticut
Hackensack, New Jersey
Mountain View, New Jersey
Newark, New Jersey
New York, New York
Port Chester, New York
Passaic, New Jersey

DATE DUE

OCT 12 '77			
AUG 4 '82			
AUG 21 '82			
MAR 20 1993			
APR 9 1993			
APR 10 1993			